Frye Salon

+ Jonathan Lasker

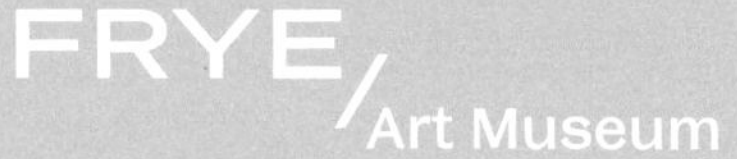

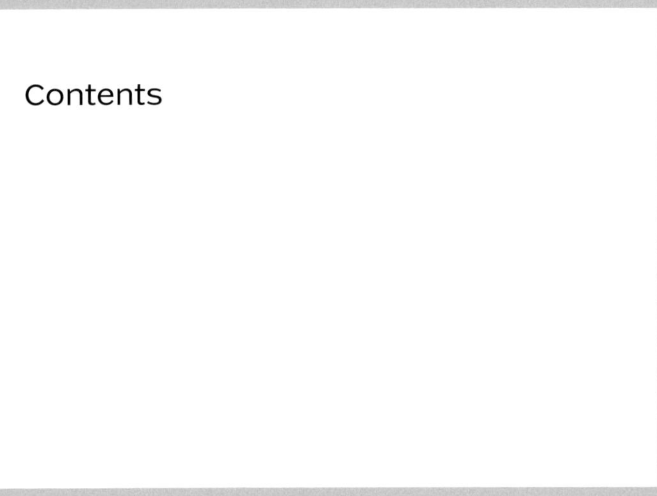

Contents

Edited by Jamilee Lacy

Frye Art Museum | 2025

Foreword

I like to think of my husband Jeff's and my involvement with art as a romance. What began twenty years ago as a curiosity deepened as we spent time together, and has since evolved into a passionate affair. Nestled under the wings of our dearest friends, we attended art fairs and galleries, dinners and museums. We read books and manifestos. Eventually, we felt ready to buy our first work.

In many ways, our collecting story echoes that of Frye Art Museum founders Charles and Emma Frye. Art resided at the center of their relationship, beginning shortly after the couple's arrival in Seattle in 1888. As Charles's meatpacking business flourished and Emma took on an active social role within the local community, their shared passion for the arts became a source of togetherness. It took them on journeys to the 1893 World's Columbian Exposition in Chicago, where they purchased their first painting, and later to Europe, where they continued to buy art. Adding a purpose-built gallery to their house, they hung their paintings in the floor to ceiling, salon-style method they experienced during their travels. The Fryes' home became a space to share their growing collection with friends and eventually the greater Seattle community. They also had a close personal connection to artist Henry Raschen (1854–1937), whose work became integral to the Fryes' collection, including his portraits of the couple (figs. 1–2).

In our scenario, Jonathan Lasker was our first true art love. As we began our collection, we knew we wanted something abstract and complex: a piece that urged us to look more closely, one that held our gaze and conveyed a sense of activity at the juncture between paint and surface. Most importantly, we desired something that brought us joy each time we encountered it. We were also seeking the art of a respected, relevant contributor to the conversation around contemporary art. We found all we were looking for in Lasker's magnificent *Ornithology, As Written for Birds* (fig. 3).

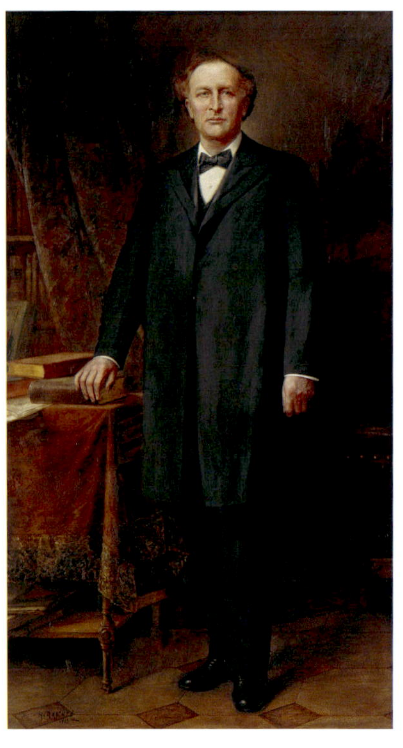

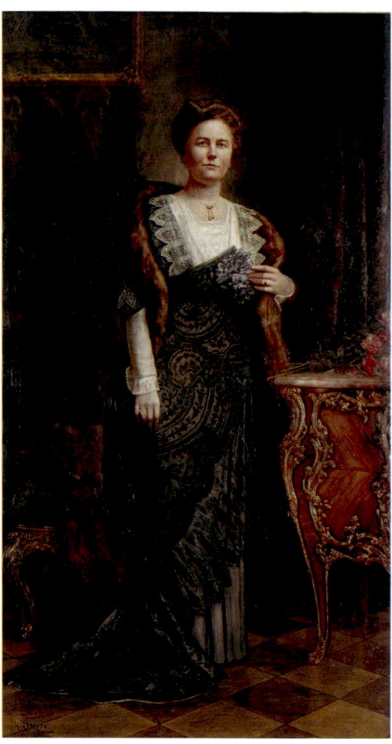

Fig. 1. Henry Raschen. *Charles H. Frye*, 1913. Oil on canvas. 85½ × 48½ in. Frye Art Museum, Founding Collection, Gift of Charles and Emma Frye, 1952.129. Photo: Spike Mafford

Fig. 2. Henry Raschen. *Emma Lamp Frye*, 1913. Oil on canvas. 85½ × 48¼ in. Frye Art Museum, Founding Collection, Gift of Charles and Emma Frye, 1952.132. Photo: Spike Mafford

The artist's simple color palette and complex, inventive visual lexicon enchanted us—though, as we subsequently learned, it was not mere abstraction. The more we were exposed to his work, the more deeply we engaged. As we became increasingly familiar with the different phases of Jonathan's work, we amassed a collection, filling it in with earlier pieces and then augmenting our holdings as his oeuvre evolved.

Much like the Fryes, the lightbulb moment in our experience as collectors came through personal connection, when we had the great honor of meeting Jonathan. He accepted our offer to show his work in an exhibition we hosted. Speaking with a small group of Seattle friends and art museum patrons, he explained how he is not an abstract artist in the traditional sense. Rather, he situates an unfamiliar tableau of forms and imagery within the framework of a classical painting—one with a horizon, foreground, background, layers, and proportionality. It's no wonder that *Admirable Stasis*

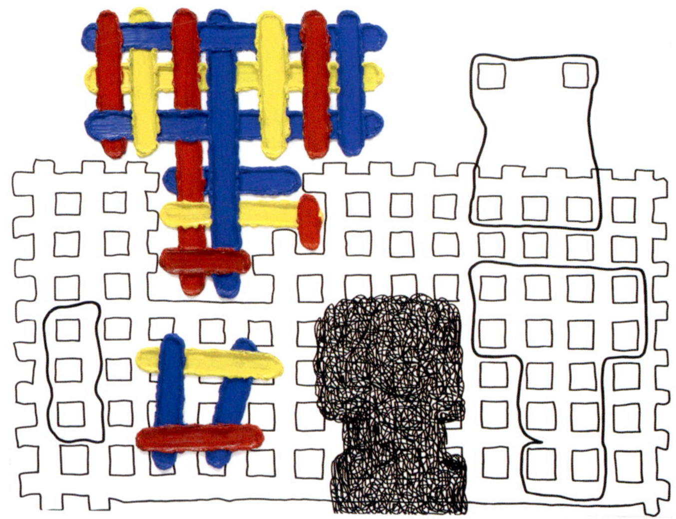

Fig. 3. Jonathan Lasker. *Ornithology, As Written for Birds*, 2003. Oil on linen. 63 × 84 in. © Jonathan Lasker. Courtesy of the artist; Greene Naftali, New York; Thaddaeus Ropac, Paris; and Timothy Taylor, New York

(fig. 4) reminds me of a portrait; *Canaletto* (1987; fig. 3, p. 15) of a map; and *Domestic Setting with Post-Partum Anxiety* (1999) of a mother, empty and uncertain.

Jonathan's art requires us to impose our own meanings onto the worlds he creates. His cerebral approach invites us to participate in the intellectual tensions embedded in his imagery. His paintings stimulate elements drawn from our own minds and our own personal narratives. In our experience of Jonathan and his work, creativity, insights, and especially humor define the relationship.

Like so many great romances, Jeff and I had absolutely no idea that our love of and engagement with a singular work of art would turn into such enormous admiration for an artist and deep passion for the work he created over the last several decades. We certainly did not anticipate it leading to the meaningful trajectory of our married life's vocation as collectors of modern and contemporary art, one that reflects the spirit of Charles and Emma Frye. It is our great privilege both to share

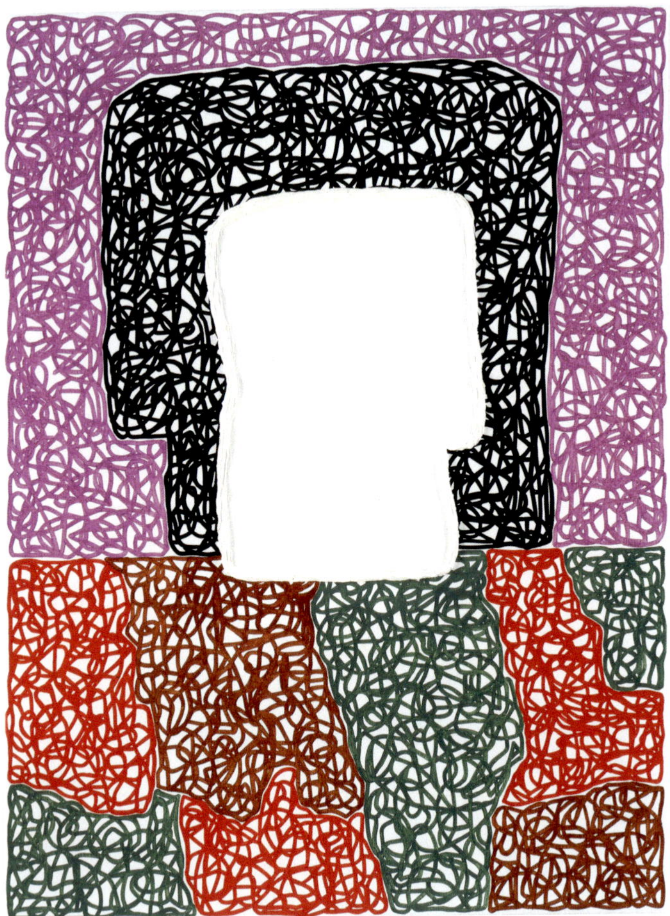

Fig. 4. Jonathan Lasker. *Admirable Stasis*, 2006. Oil on linen. 40 × 30 in. © Jonathan Lasker. Courtesy of the artist; Greene Naftali, New York; Thaddaeus Ropac, Paris; and Timothy Taylor, New York

with Seattle the visionary work of an artist we admire and to see our collecting story intersect with the Frye couple's in the dynamic exhibition *Frye Salon + Jonathan Lasker*. For all that, Jonathan, we thank you.

Judy Greenstein

Introduction: An Abbreviated History of Rebel Painters

Jamilee Lacy

Painting dominates the history of art. A powerful medium for telling stories, proliferating ideas, and continually captivating large swaths of culture, the discipline and its practitioners naturally change over time. Yet one thing remains constant: rebellious painters. They move the discourse forward, changing to meet head-on the prevailing issues of the times. Albeit with dramatically different styles, rebel painters constitute *Frye Salon + Jonathan Lasker*. This unique exhibition juxtaposes the works of Munich Secession artists and other late nineteenth- and early twentieth-century painters with those of one of Postmodernism's most influential artists.

What is gained by seeing these paintings and considering these figures side by side? While the display certainly highlights divergences, it first provides several opportunities to explore how and why modern and contemporary artists consistently rejected what came before them. Secondly, the novel presentation demonstrates how painting exists as an ever-evolving dialogue, with each generation subverting existing norms and seeking new ways to express ideas, to reflect societal changes, or to push the boundaries of creativity. Finally, integrating this particular living artist's oeuvre into a historical art installation shows how painting has been and continues to be a series of rebellions that often arise from dissatisfaction with established styles, perceived limitations, or the need to break free from convention. In the truncated art histories on display in this exhibition, viewers see works from one of the first uprisings of Modern art, peppered with paintings made nearly a century later by a prominent figure of one of the most recent rebellions against an established art movement.

The conversation pursued in *Frye Salon + Jonathan Lasker* starts in the late nineteenth century, around the time the museum's founders, Charles and Emma Frye, began collecting art. Industrialization and rapid social change were reshaping the social, economic, and cultural landscape of Western Europe, North America, and, eventually, the world. Migration, global exchange, and new means of production transformed how people lived, worked, and traveled, broadening worldviews and introducing new ideas. This era saw the birth of Modernism and, in turn, Modern art, during which many artists created paintings based on their own experiences and viewpoints. The children of German immigrants, the Fryes were first drawn not to Modern art, but to variations of European and American Romantic Realism, an artistic approach that merges the emotional intensity and idealism of Romanticism with the observational precision of realism.

Although Romantic Realism shares elements with Modern art, such as an emphasis on individual perspective, emotional depth, and psychological themes, its practitioners did not seek to radically transform the way paintings are made. In 1892, however, the Munich Secession emerged: a breakaway movement that rejected the academy-trained realism of the Munich school, one of the most significant centers of academic painting in nineteenth-century Europe. Many people today are more familiar with the Vienna Secession and its most famous member, Gustav Klimt. However, the Munich Secession came first and enormously influenced later splinter movements. The Secession painters ultimately helped lay the foundation for twentieth-century Modernism.

The Secession movement absorbed influences from Symbolism, German Impressionism, and *Jugendstil*,[1] marking a stark departure from the Munich school's classical realism. Further influenced by Sigmund Freud's *The Interpretation of Dreams* (1899) and its elevation of the subconscious mind, these artists instead played with real-world space, using foregrounds, backgrounds, framing devices, and more to explore dreams and personal iconography as avenues for depicting subjective experiences and diverse beliefs. Yet with no defined style or aesthetic rules to adhere to, artists in the group experimented in different ways. For Fritz von Uhde, the rebellion against tradition meant a lighter palette based on observation of nature and a more direct expression of emotion. Some members focused on technique, as seen in the impressionistic brushstrokes of Uhde or the flattening of forms by Oskar Zwintscher. Others incorporated nontraditional subject matter, such as the symbolist expression of idealized, dark sexuality that appears in Franz von Stuck's *Die Sünde* (Sin) (fig. 1).

Eschewing the aesthetic uniformity typical of most art movements, the Munich Secession illustrated a variety of

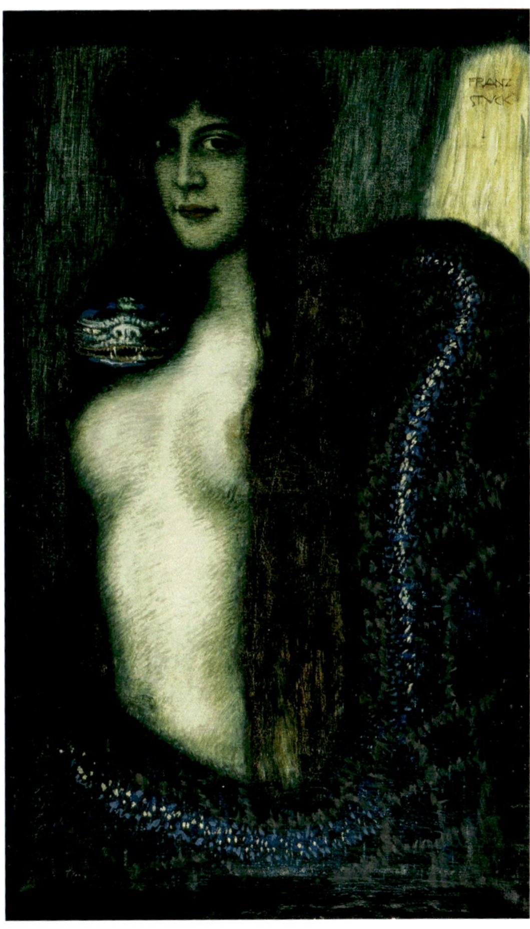

Fig. 1. Franz von Stuck. *Die Sünde* (Sin), ca. 1908. Tempera on canvas. 34⅞ × 21⅝ in. Frye Art Museum, Founding Collection, Gift of Charles and Emma Frye, 1952.169. Photo: Spike Mafford

avant-garde techniques and philosophies that impressed *The New York Times* when the Metropolitan Museum of Art exhibited Secessionist work there in 1909 (fig. 2). *The Times* praised "the impulsive, energetic, and extremely various art" in the exhibition and described it as "a force to be reckoned with," noting that it showed "how far individualism may be carried."[2]

Informed both by the exhibition at the Met and the drama unfolding between these artistic rebels and their more traditional counterparts, the extensive German holdings within *Frye Salon* consist of works by such leading Munich Secessionist painters as Franz von Stuck, Ludwig Dill, Max Liebermann, and Hugo von Habermann. It also features works by artists who maintained their association with the Munich school and the

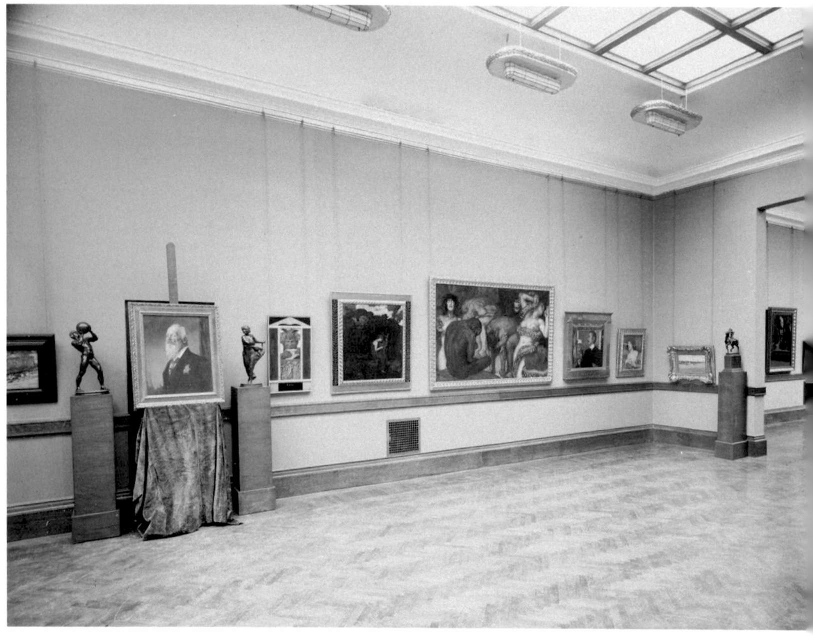

Munich Artists' Association and adhered strictly to principles of realist painting, including figures like Franz von Lenbach, Friedrich August von Kaulbach, Wilhelm Leibl, and Franz von Defregger.

Fig. 2. Installation view of *Contemporary German Art*, The Metropolitan Museum of Art, New York, January 4–February 22, 1909. © The Metropolitan Museum of Art, New York. Image courtesy Art Resource, NY

Modern art underwent radical transformations for the next seventy-five years, shifting from representational forms to increasing abstraction and conceptual experimentation. Movements like Cubism, Futurism, and Expressionism broke away from perspective and narrative, followed by Dada and Surrealism, which embraced chance, irrationality, and the subconscious. The mid-twentieth century brought Abstract Expressionism, wherein artists like Jackson Pollock and Mark Rothko prioritized gesture, emotion, and color fields. At the same time, the 1960s and 1970s saw painting heavily influenced by movements like Pop art, Minimalism, and Conceptual art, which broadly prioritized ideas or reduced art to fundamental forms.

Jeff and Judy Greenstein, a Seattle-area couple collecting art a century after the Fryes, have committed to acquiring works that tell the story of artists rebelling and establishing new modes of abstract art in the latter half of the twentieth century. Jonathan Lasker's work prominently features in that story and within their collection, on loan to the Frye on the occasion of *Frye Salon + Jonathan Lasker*.

Lasker emerged in the late 1970s and early 1980s, when many artists felt beleaguered by Minimalism's overly rigid and impersonal approach. This movement, which began in the 1960s, emphasized simplicity, repetition, and the idea that art should not be self-referential—free from narrative, symbols, or personal expression. While partly a reaction against the emotional intensity of Abstract Expressionism, some Postmodern artists found Minimalism limiting and questioned its claims to objectivity and neutrality. As a response, a new generation of artists embraced complexity, irony, and subjectivity. Movements like Neo-Expressionism, Conceptual art, and Appropriation art deliberately reintroduced storytelling, humor, pastiche, and references to mass culture. Artists like Jean-Michel Basquiat and Julian Schnabel created expressive, layered paintings, while others, like Barbara Kruger and Sherrie Levine, used appropriation and text to critique the idea of originality.

Lasker, too, understood Minimalism as a creative dead end. His early paintings (fig. 3) challenged its austerity by reintroducing expressive gestures, psychological depth, and idiosyncratic imagery into abstraction. While Minimalism emphasized impersonal, geometric forms and completely rejected narrative, Lasker subverted these ideas by embracing hand-drawn, almost crude lines, layered compositions, and symbolic motifs that suggest meaning beyond pure form. His later works (fig. 4) build on personalized symbology and favor clean lines and industrial precision yet maintain textural diversity to emphasize the act and materiality of painting itself.

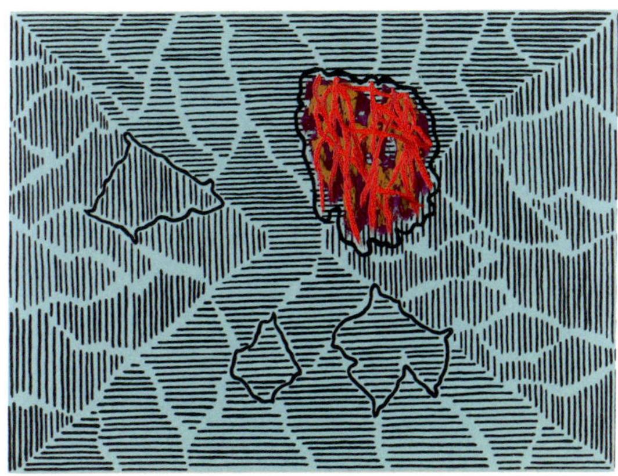

Fig. 3. Jonathan Lasker. *Canaletto*, 1987. Oil on linen. 52 × 72 in. © Jonathan Lasker. Courtesy of the artist; Greene Naftali, New York; Thaddaeus Ropac, Paris; and Timothy Taylor, New York. Photo: Elisabeth Bernstein

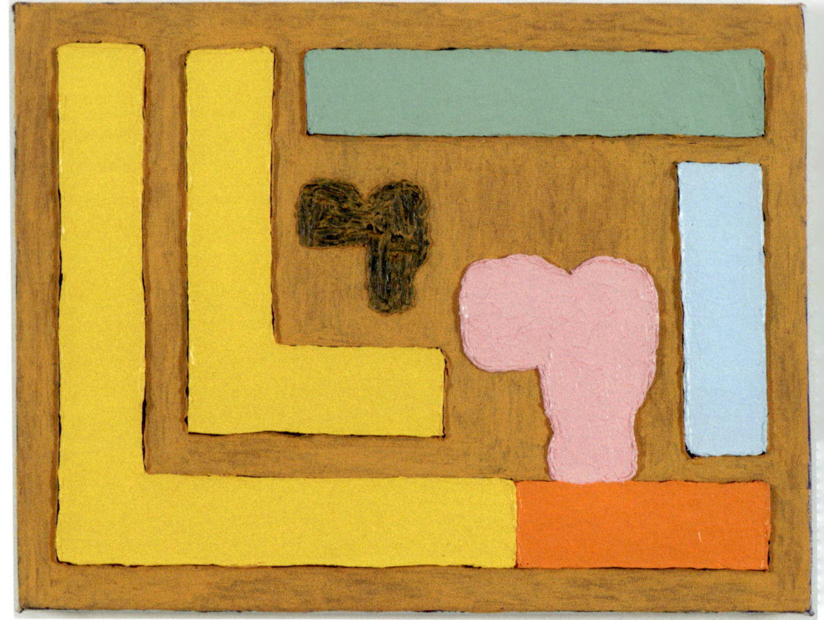

Fig. 4. Jonathan Lasker. *Cult of Security*, 2020. Oil on linen. 12 × 16 in. © Jonathan Lasker. Courtesy of the artist; Greene Naftali, New York; Thaddaeus Ropac, Paris; and Timothy Taylor, New York. Photo: Zeshan Ahmed

Lasker's rejection of Minimalism also meant that he opposed its core principles, which emphasized simplicity, the visual absence of the handmade, and the removal of subjective meaning from art. Artists associated with the movement like Donald Judd and Frank Stella sought to strip art down to its essential forms, using industrial materials and geometric structure to emphasize pure, non-referential visual experience. Lasker, by contrast, deliberately reintroduced elements that Minimalism sought to erase—gesture; nods to painterly traditions like foreground, background, and horizon lines; and a willingness to playfully engage with meaning beyond pure form. Instead of reducing painting to basic shapes and colors, he embraced complexity, creating works that challenge the viewer with ambiguous imagery that hovers between abstraction and representation. Rejecting the pursuit of clarity and order, Lasker alludes to yet cleverly bypasses conventional compositional rules. The results create visual puzzles where repetition and recognizable elements seem to appear without fully resolving, encouraging the viewer to interpret pictorial language with partial fluency. Welcoming visual ambiguity and subjective interpretation,

Lasker produces paintings that suggest—but never completely define—letters, figures, landscapes, and whatever else the imagination conjures.

Ultimately, *Frye Salon + Jonathan Lasker* underscores a crucial truth about the evolution of painting: It endures through a continuous cycle of rebellion and reinvention. From the Munich Secessionists' break with academic realism to Lasker's defiance of Minimalism, artists have consistently sought to upend the norms and expand the boundaries of the medium. This exhibition serves as a reminder that art, especially painting, is not a static tradition but a dynamic and ever-changing force driven by a restless pursuit of new ways to see, think, and create.

Notes

1. This decorative style (translated as "youth-style") arose in late nineteenth- and early twentieth-century Germany and bears relation to Art Nouveau.

2. "German Art Shown At Metropolitan. Entire Field of Modern Painting from Lenbach to Menzel on Exhibition. Are Tastefully Selected. Cream of the Works of Modern German Artists Show Struggle Between Younger and Older Generation," *The New York Times*, April 1, 1909, quoted in Jo-Anne Birnie Danzker, "The Munich Secession in America: The Collections of Hugo Reisinger, Josef Stránský, Charles and Emma Frye," in *Secession 1892–1914*, ed. Michael Buhrs (Museum Villa Stuck, Munich, 2008), 281.

Jonathan Lasker and Jamilee Lacy in Conversation

Jamilee Lacy: I'm thrilled to interview you for this book. I first encountered your work as an art-school freshman in the early 2000s, nearly twenty-five years after you started making paintings. Here we are another couple decades on, and I'm wondering, how did the artist life begin for you, especially given that you didn't go to art school right away?

Jonathan Lasker: True, I didn't go to college right after high school, but regardless, I managed to avoid the [Vietnam] draft and pursued becoming a musician. I say "pursued becoming" because in all sincerity, I did not have the skills to be a good musician. My ideas were good, but my ears were faulty. Nonetheless, this pursuit embarked me on an odyssey of almost four years of travel in Europe. Only the first of those years entailed actively trying to get into a band in England. After candidly acknowledging that I stunk, I decided to travel until I determined my future. First landing in Hamburg, Germany, I began my vagabond lifestyle. Initially, I lived and worked there, but gradually I migrated until I had spent a considerable amount of time in many of the countries of Europe and North Africa—and gained fluency in German—before returning to America.

When I moved to New York City, I had just turned twenty-six. By that time, I had decided on a medium of expression that suited my skills—namely, painting—as I had always had an adept hand in painting and drawing.

After years of experimenting as a traveler in life, I decided to do something I believed I could do well, and I was not about to be dissuaded. First, I took evening classes at the School of Visual Arts while working in retail as an assistant buyer. Then, I embarked on a very big joke: I enrolled at Cal Arts [California Institute of the Arts], of all places, to become a painter!

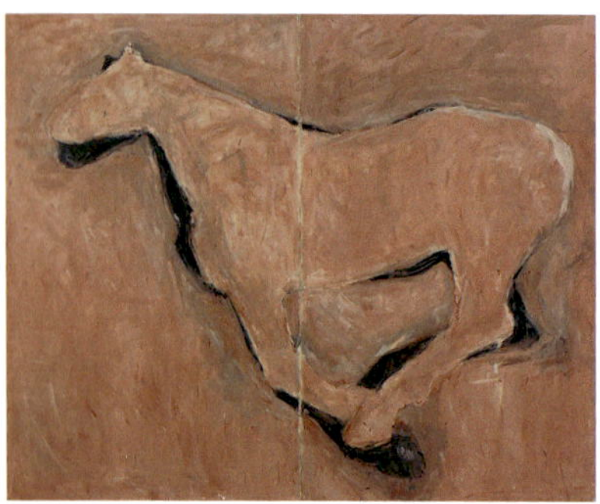
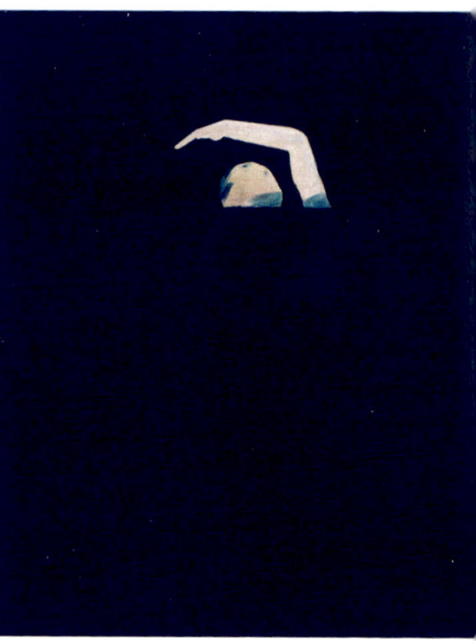

Lacy: When you started college in the mid-1970s, Minimalism had been going strong for a decade or so, and painting was considered dead by the art world. At that time, Cal Arts was an institution with strong ties to the birth of Conceptualism, which prioritizes an artwork's idea over any technical or material concerns. It must have been an interesting place for a young painter. Who influenced you, there and beyond?

From left:
Fig. 1. Susan Rothenberg. *Cabin Fever*, 1976. Acrylic and tempera on canvas. 67 × 84⅛ in. Collection of the Modern Art Museum of Fort Worth, Museum purchase, Sid W. Richardson Foundation Endowment Fund and an Anonymous Donor. © The Estate of Susan Rothenberg / Artists Rights Society (ARS), NY

Fig. 2. Robert Moskowitz. *Swimmer*, 1977. Dry pigment, oil, and graphite pencil on canvas. 90 × 74¾ in. Whitney Museum of American Art, New York, NY; gift of Jennifer Bartlett, 82.9. © 2025 Robert Moskowitz / Licensed by VAGA at Artists Rights Society (ARS), NY. Digital image © Whitney Museum of American Art / Licensed by Scala / Art Resource, NY

Lasker: Significant to me personally was my professor at Cal Arts, Susan Rothenberg. Susan gave me vital support at a critical moment when I did the first couple of paintings in my body of work. At the time, she was trying to make an artistic exit from her horse paintings and doing conflated, intertwined heads and hands. It is a really good series, and I'll always remember seeing them then at art college before the broader public did. The horse paintings, however, are more negative/positive and figure/ground works and extremely powerful pieces, both because of the nature of the images and also because of the primal expressiveness of the subject (fig. 1).

That group of artists in the 1970s, the so-called New Image painters (due to the eponymous exhibition at the Whitney [Museum of American Art] in 1978) also includes Robert Moskowitz, who centered iconic forms: the Flatiron Building, the rear fin of a Cadillac, the Twin Towers, the head and uplifted arm of a woman swimmer who is either robustly exercising or frantically trying not to drown (fig. 2). All these paintings by Moskowitz displayed a solitary, isolated figure seemingly in existential crisis, as did Denise Green's *Chair* or her *Longhouse* paintings (also in the Whitney's *New Image Painting* show). These pictures seem to signal the survival of the painted figure at a moment when painting altogether was in doubt. The figures are surrounded by atmospheric grounds poised to engulf them.

The painter Malcolm Morley stands out most in this regard. The painterly disruptions in his work are a kind of figure/ground event (fig. 3). He would take a fully rendered photorealist image and mar it with a painterly mark or large dripping *X*. I think Malcolm was and is a very underrated artist, specifically regarding figure/ground relationships. This effect in his work has always fascinated me. Most viewers would probably not expect my feeling of

Fig. 3. Malcolm Morley. *Mariner*, 1998. Oil paint on canvas. 116⅛ × 147½ in. Tate, Purchased with assistance from the American Fund for the Tate Gallery, the Friends of the Tate Gallery and the Evelyn, Lady Downshire's Fund 2001. © The Estate of Malcolm Morley. Photo: Tate

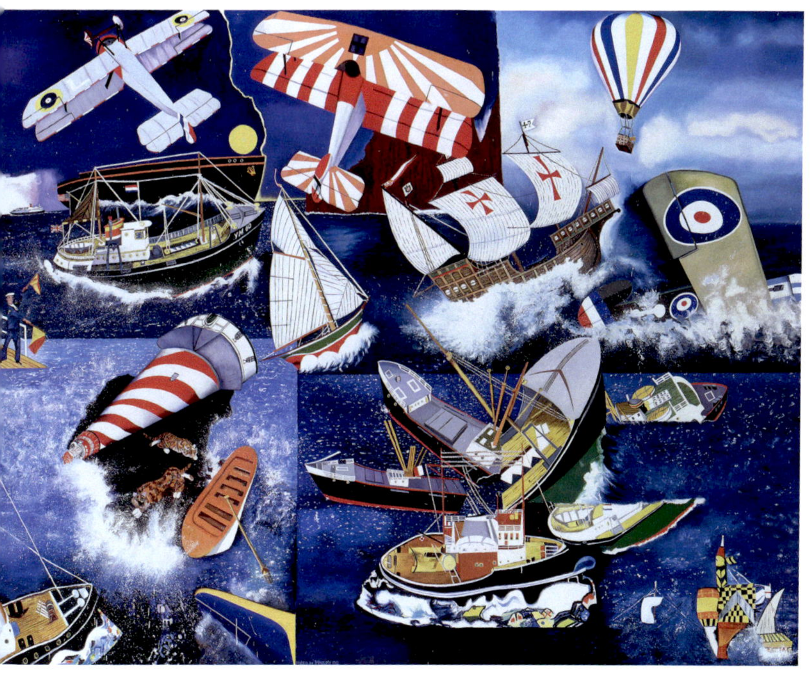

connectedness with Morley since our works really don't look alike, but there is also a willful disfigurement in my work. I am most compelled by Morley's use of grounds, which are not conceived with passive motives. Generally, the more resistant the so-called ground is, the more tension it endows the painting.

As for other influences, my work couldn't exist without the entire history of art rolling around in my head. From my youth onwards, Abstract Expressionists like Willem de Kooning and Franz Kline left a resonant mark on me. Since I use visual tropes in my work to form dialogue, the formal vocabulary of other artists can sometimes emerge in aspects of one picture or another. For instance, I have used Joan Mitchell's painting style for one or two overall backgrounds in 1970s paintings such as *Bayou* (1978). Larry Rivers's approach, freeing lines from the edges of their forms, finds its way into my work, not quotationally, but generally.

Lacy: It seems so natural to me, in this moment, to situate your work within a variety of movements and styles, spanning Pattern and Decoration [P&D] and New Image painting to the conceptual art of Daniel Buren. It sits just as well with that of painters, like Charline von Heyl and Rebecca Morris, among others, who made their names a generation or two after you.

Lasker: It's funny that it seems natural to you today, but it wasn't always so natural for viewers. For many people, it created an uneasy feeling, and their judgment of my paintings' palettes and patterns as "bad taste" often went against me. To me, risking bad taste—or even making art on the edge of kitsch—could enable a work to break new ground. Somehow, this risk very often made a painting resonate for me.

Also, the Pattern and Decoration movement was prominent in the 1970s when I was forming my work at Cal Arts. I started out making pattern paintings before finding that laying a white form on top of the pattern, with an off-register black line painted into it, formed a very interesting effect. So, pattern painters like Robert Zakanitch and Valerie Jaudon (now a good friend) (fig. 4) were influential to me. In general, P&D is regarded as a minor movement, which made it all the more useful as an influence. If you want to do an original work, seek minor influences. Those

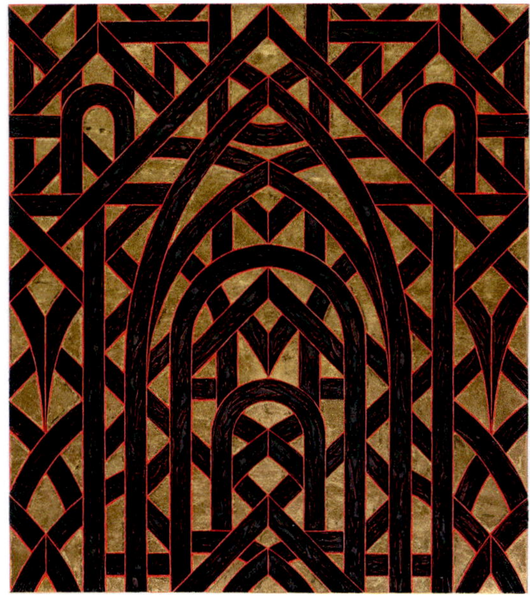

Fig. 4. Valerie Jaudon. *Gold Leaf, Red & Black*, 1981. Etching and aquatint with gold leaf and varnish additions. Plate 26⅛ × 23⅞ in. Publisher & Printer: Aeropress, New York. Edition: 12. The Museum of Modern Art/ New York, NY; John B. Turner Fund. © 2025 Valerie Jaudon / Licensed by VAGA at Artists Rights Society (ARS), NY. Digital image © The Museum of Modern Art / Licensed by Scala / Art Resource, NY

artists are always touching on something that reverberates in a way others are not seeing.

In a way, I feel happy to have begun painting at the time I did, even if it was very challenging. I think my generation of painters will have a much more lasting effect than they are given credit for. They mostly started working at the time when painting was disallowed, and they all sought different ways to validate it. Elizabeth Murray, Mary Heilmann, Tom Nozkowski, David Salle, Philip Taaffe, David Reed, Peter Halley, and numerous others of my time renewed abstract painting each in their own way.

Lacy: You're known for having created your own kind of visual language, including but not limited to biomorphic forms, thick black lines, layered scribbles, and combinations of flat and textured surfaces. The language becomes especially evident in works like *The Universal Frame of Reference* (fig. 5), which still seems akin to much older paintings such as *Psychic Governance* (fig. 6). How do you maintain a language like this over such a long period of time and continue to generate new works from it?

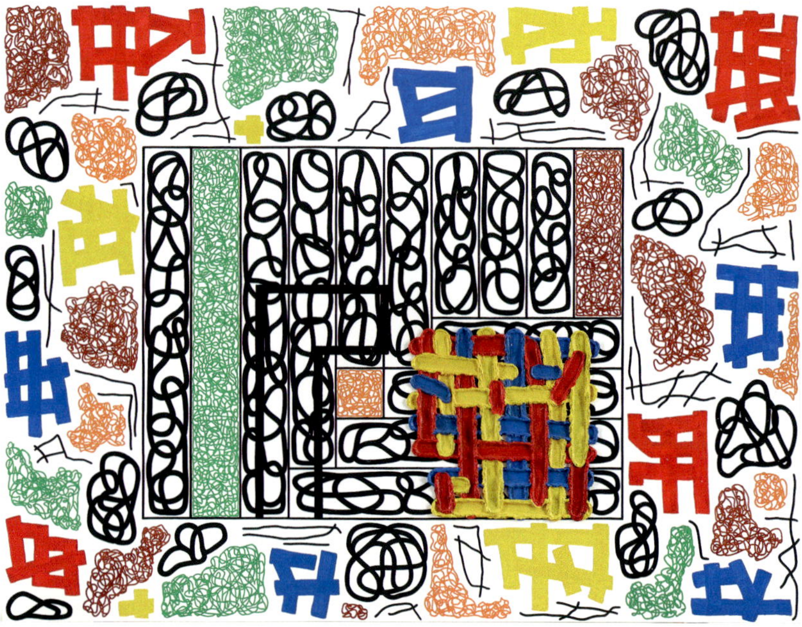

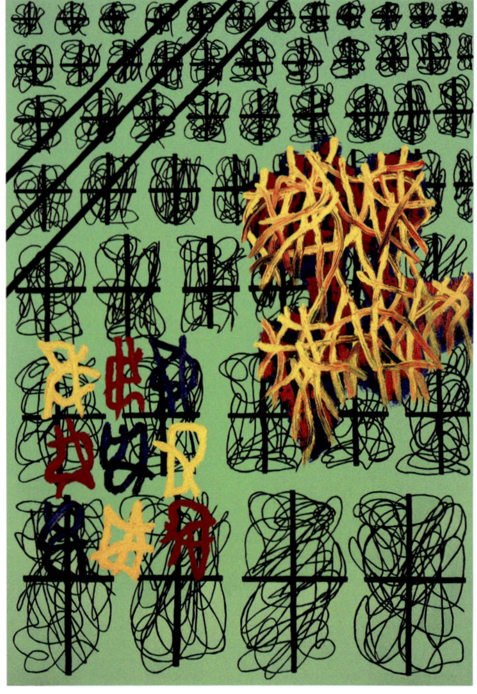

Above:
Fig. 5. Jonathan Lasker. *The Universal Frame of Reference*, 2014. Oil on linen. 90 × 120 in. National Gallery of Canada, Ottawa, Purchased 2016. © Jonathan Lasker. Courtesy of the artist; Greene Naftali, New York; Thaddaeus Ropac, Paris; and Timothy Taylor, New York

At left:
Fig. 6. Jonathan Lasker. *Psychic Governance*, 1989. Oil on linen. 84 × 60 in. Private collection, Belgium. © Jonathan Lasker. Courtesy of the artist; Greene Naftali, New York; Thaddaeus Ropac, Paris; and Timothy Taylor, New York

Lasker: I liken my relationship to my body of work to a prospector's with his source of ore, which he discovered and developed into a mine. So long as each return trip can reward me with images that can be turned into pictures I haven't made before, I continue digging. The shift from one work to the next might be only a variation, but sometimes it can bring a paradigmatic epiphany. For example, I totally understand why you see a conversance between *Psychic Governance* and *The Universal Frame of Reference*, which were painted with a twenty-five-year time gap between them. There is a convergence of the visual tropes (signs) in both pictures, but to me, a seismic spatial shift separates these two pictures.

The Universal Frame of Reference was a new development for me in its composition: The signs from the inner picture plane form the outer patterned picture plane. By setting it all on one canvas, the work challenges the boundaries of what we call a "composed picture." So, this example makes two points for me: One, that the mine can still reward me. However, point two speaks to the question of repetition; this painting suggests there are limitations to perpetually mining the same quarry. Although I did a few variations, such as the related *The Eternal Present* (2016) and numerous small works, the original *The Universal Frame of Reference* is a great painting because of its perfect execution of a system. If one followed its rules, it would always make an exciting painting—unless one used the same devices *ad nauseam*, which I never did. I simply didn't want to take a group of great paintings and run them into the ground. That said, maybe the world could take another twenty or so of these paintings and be happy with them, but the limits are finite. I would certainly never do a show with only these paintings. When perfection is repeated, it can become trite. It's like the title. I originally thought to call it *A Universal Frame of Reference*, but I knew it had to be *The Universal Frame of Reference*. You can do a few variations of such a picture, but after that, it really takes nerve to do more.

Nonetheless, spontaneity exists, albeit frozen, in my work. The rapidly drawn and painstakingly painted scribbles are even more affecting because of their fossilization. The passage of time distances the nervous activity of the hand doing the scribble from the viewer's reception of the image.

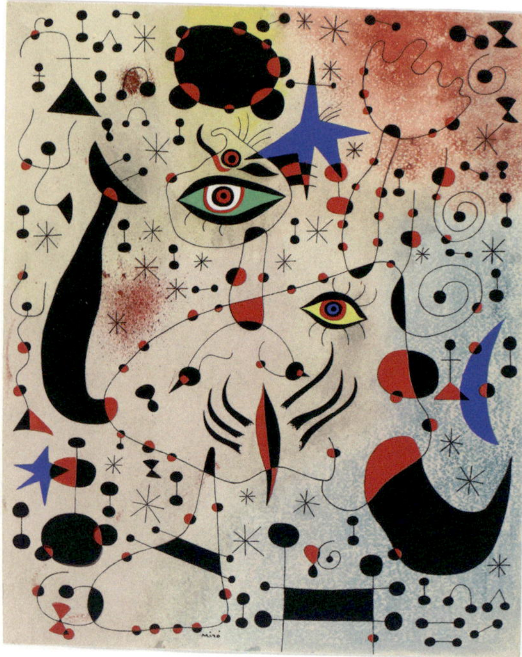

Fig. 7. Joan Miró. *19. Chiffres et constellations amoureux d'une femme* [A Woman's Amourous Numbers and Constellations], from the portfolio *Constellations*, 1941–1959. Collotype on velin. 14 × 17 in. Musée National d'Art Moderne/ Centre Georges Pompidou/ Paris/France, AM1999-4(20). © Successió Miró / Artists Rights Society (ARS), NY / ADAGP, Paris 2025. Digital Image © CNAC/ MNAM, Dist. RMN-Grand Palais / Art Resource, NY. Photo: Audrey Laurans

I set something aside when I feel that I've depleted the subject matter of what that type of picture can open up for me, and I return to it when I realize it still has unrealized pictures in it, that there is simply more to say.

Lacy: And people like me puzzle over and fall in love with the recurring imagery. (I especially keep coming back for the biomorphic forms.) What sustains your interest?

Lasker: My love for biomorphic forms does not really go so deep. I inherited these forms as part of a common abstract-painting vocabulary that comes from artists like André Masson, Joan Miró, and William Baziotes. Unto themselves, they are convenient tropes that symbolize the Jungian archetypal subconscious, particularly when conflated with geometric abstraction. I probably find Miró's use of this type of form most cogent (fig. 7).

Lacy: Your color palettes reoccur and are quite bold yet still relatively limited. To me, your colors often look chemical,

almost fluorescent. What's your secret to making them vibrate so?

Lasker: I am not doing anything particular to the colors to enhance their vibrancy. However, I rarely use more than six colors in any one canvas. Most paintings have four or five. So, the integrity of each color stays intact. Also, a lot of what happens within the work relates to a Josef Albers–like juxtaposition of color.

Lacy: Since you're divulging secrets, can you tell me how you achieve the big swaths of impasto in many of the paintings (fig. 8)?

Lasker: This question always surprises me because the method seems easy to me, but of course I am the person who developed the method. So, for me it is easy. Simply load a large brush with a large amount of paint and press down on the paint as you draw it out. Reload the brush as needed. The pressure of the brush helps form a full edge with a relatively thin stroke center. The cast light of the edge enhances the feeling of volume.

Lacy: While your overall body of work is abstract, the compositional and formal logic you employ—rendering object-like forms in spaces with discernable foregrounds and

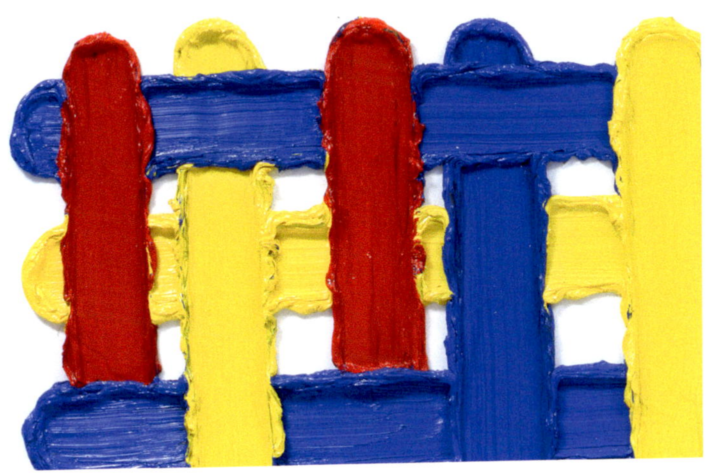

Fig. 8. Jonathan Lasker. *Ornithology, As Written for Birds* (detail), 2003. Oil on linen. 63 × 84 in. © Jonathan Lasker. Courtesy of the artist; Greene Naftali, New York; Thaddaeus Ropac, Paris; and Timothy Taylor, New York

backgrounds—conjures the narrative techniques of genre-based pictures. What inspired you to work this way?

Lasker: This is a little hard to answer, but I do try to anticipate whether my pictures will be read as I wish them to be. Take the headlike forms in my pictures, for example. I'm aware that people often puzzle over whether they are heads or not. Just so long as they puzzle, I feel the forms are acceptable to use. If that questioning departed from how those forms are viewed, I would stop having them in my pictures. I really don't want viewers to lock into a firm narrative picture.

From the beginning, I wanted my paintings to become as pictorial as possible. I started painting at a time when the picture plane needed to be filled back in, after Minimalism, and after it was discredited by Conceptualism. Although my forms are not recognizable, they do act as things in real-world space and are "actors" in a constructed space that is, at times, like a proscenium stage. So, if these paintings are abstract, it is not a pure abstraction.

Also, my work was always intended as a means of regenerating painting, and as such, I felt it needed to be metaphoric. This, to me, was the only way out of the cul-de-sac of pure abstraction: an imageless canvas that reiterated the physical properties of its own structure, such as those by Frank Stella or Robert Ryman. I like the work of both artists, but I didn't see them as models for future creativity.

Lacy: Does your understanding of the work change when you see it outside the studio? Or when you see it in conversation with works of other artists?

Lasker: My feelings about my work are generally exclusive of the environments they are put into. They are more about how and why I came to create them.

Lacy: You've long had a studio in SoHo, and your work has figured prominently in the last few decades of painting coming out of New York. But now you're working much of the year from a new studio in Munich. How does this impact your studio practice or production?

Lasker: Over the years I've had a lot of painting studios in different locations, so I'm not now feeling especially overwhelmed with a sense of dislocation. But being in Munich has helped me initiate a new series of small canvases with gestural, headlike linear drawings overlayed on top of each other and overlayed again with thick, pastel-colored forms drawn into with black paint. If my paintings often refer to different genres like landscape or still life, then these paintings can be seen as a kind of portraiture. So, being in a new studio here and beginning again provided an openness for this to happen. This is a good event that can happen in a new place.

Lacy: The museum is showing some of your paintings within *Frye Salon*, a floor to ceiling display of nineteenth- and twentieth-century realist and Romantic paintings, each of which exists to convey some sort of narrative. I'm excited to see the pictorial tensions and, perhaps, harmonies that spring forth. What could go wrong?

Lasker: Quite a lot could go wrong. My paintings already have a lot of conflicting elements within themselves that are set against one another. They are actually known for this type of visual argumentation. So, inviting additional interference from outside the picture plane could short-circuit the viewer's response.

Also, when I hang a show, I seek to do it with a minimum of paintings and a maximum of space between them. My paintings are not meant to be crowded.

Lacy: Given the dense installation of paintings in *Frye Salon*, your paintings will have less breathing room than you're used to . . . But what could go right?

Lasker: What could go right is that the genre aspect of my works could come forward and the pictorial quality could become apparent, meaning that although their forms are abstract, they can also be construed as landscapes, still lifes, or portraits, which is why I started to do them initially—to get out of the dead end of Minimalism!

Lacy: Hear hear.

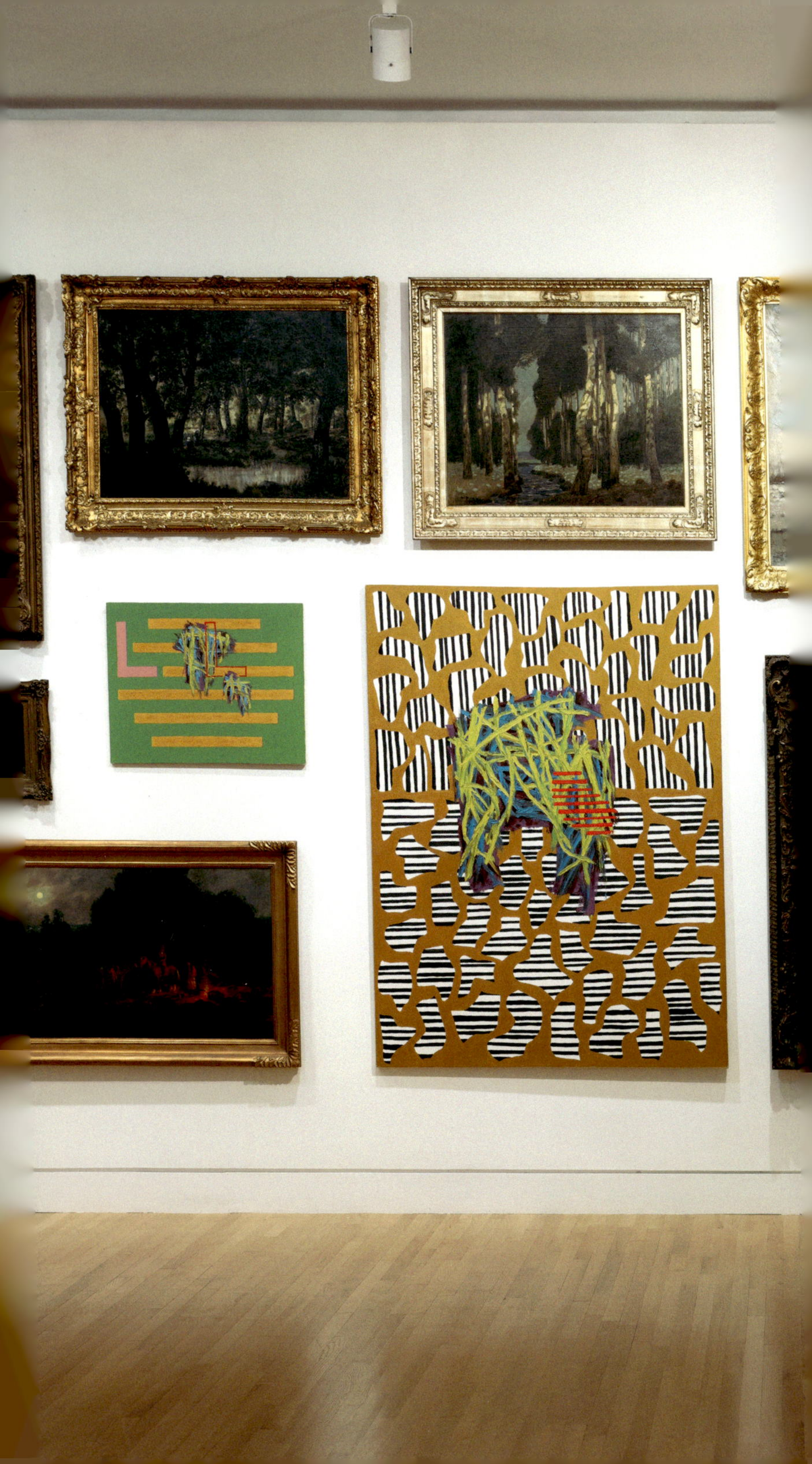

Plates

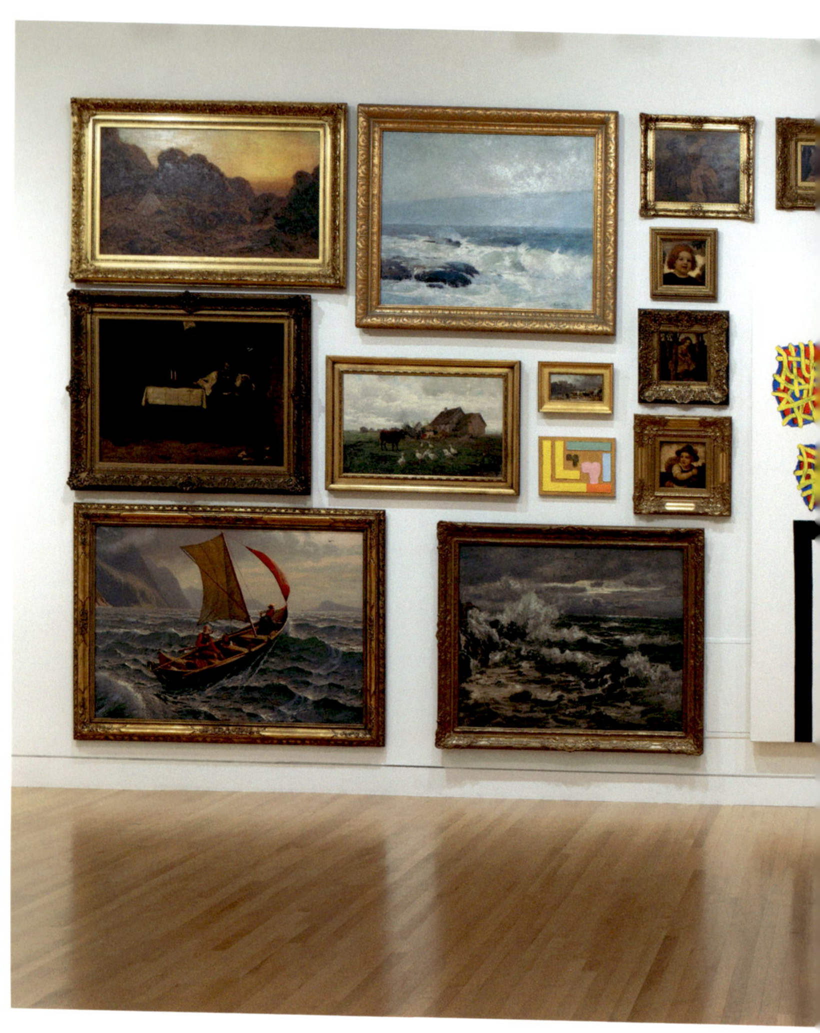

All installation photographs of *Frye Salon + Jonathan Lasker* by Jueqian Fang

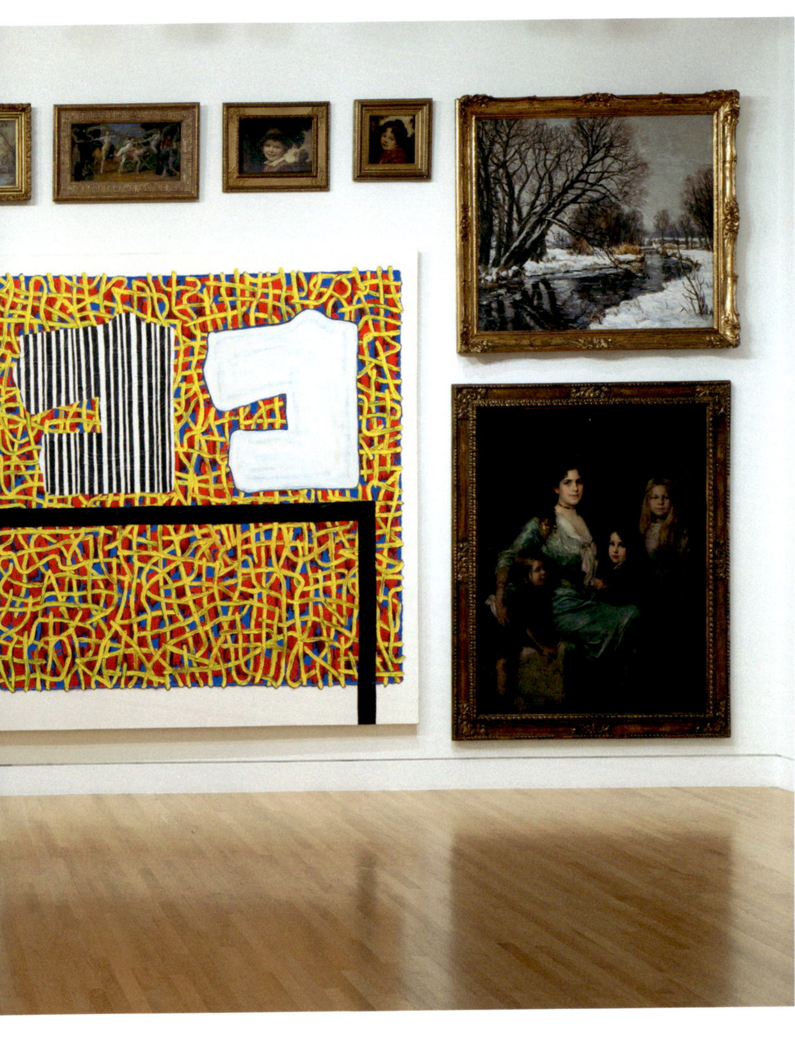

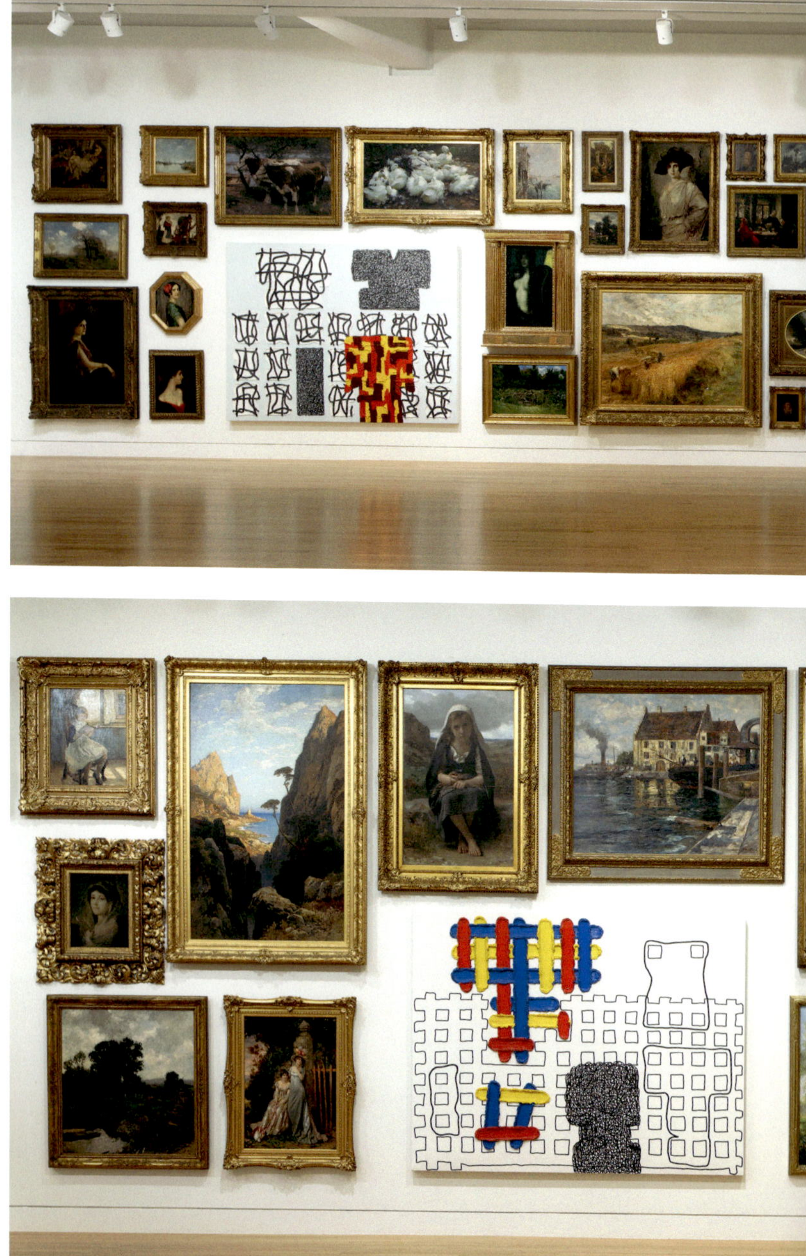

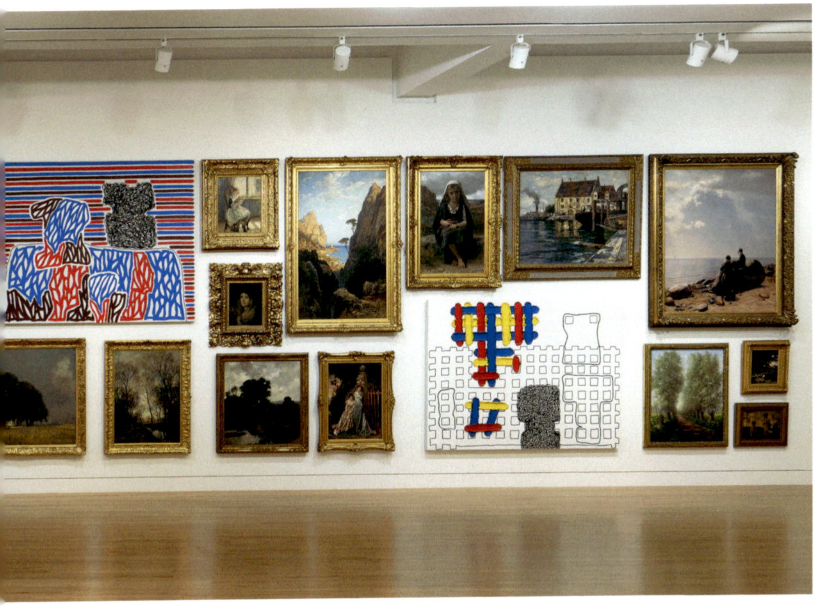

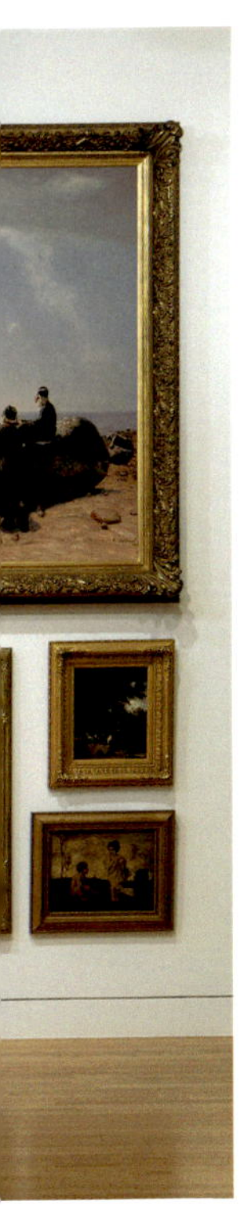

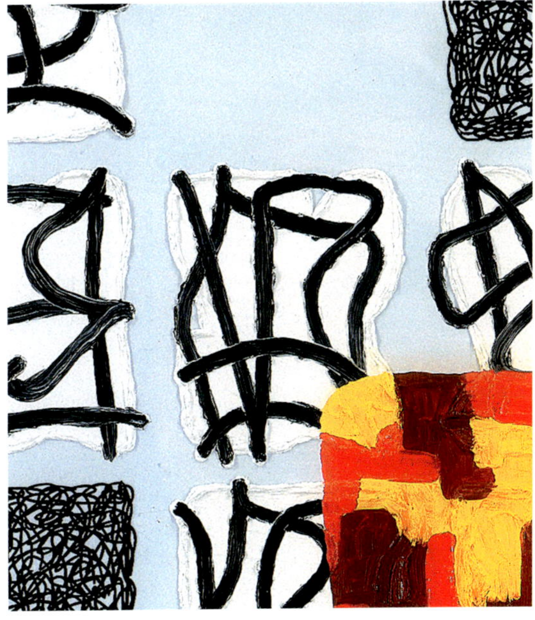

Jonathan Lasker. *The Discontinuous Self* (detail), 2000. Oil on linen. 75 × 100 in. Courtesy of the artist; Greene Naftali, New York; Thaddaeus Ropac, Paris; and Timothy Taylor, New York

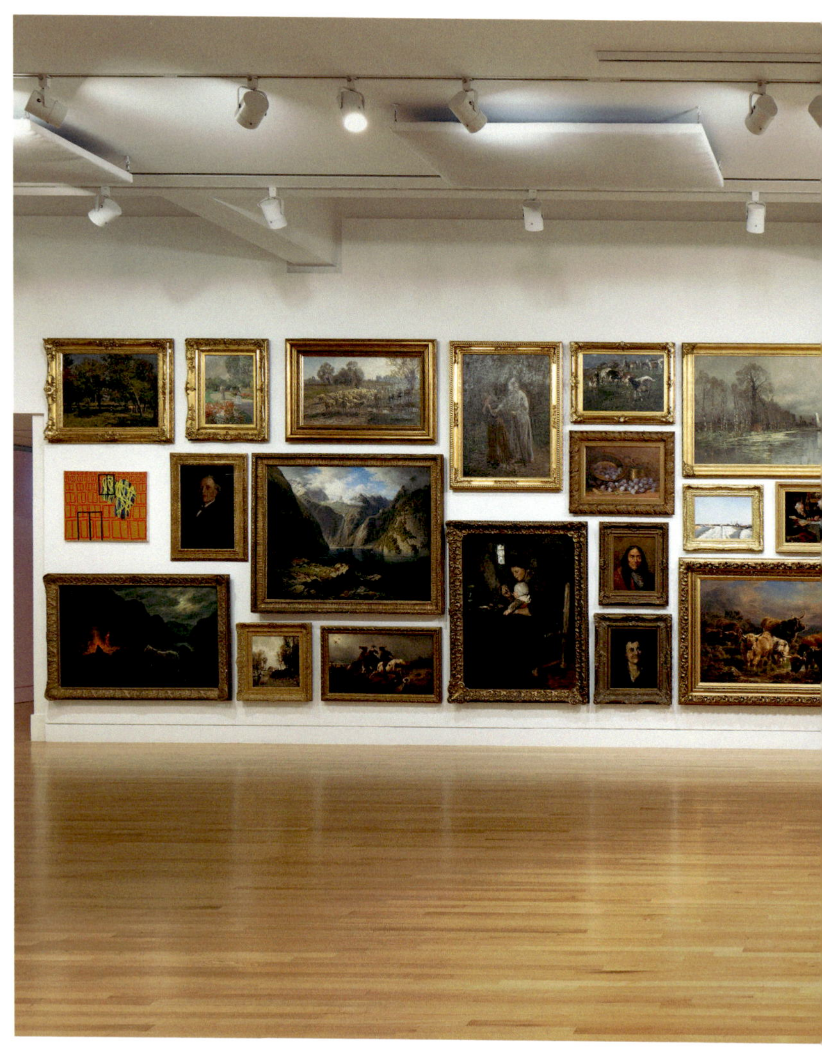

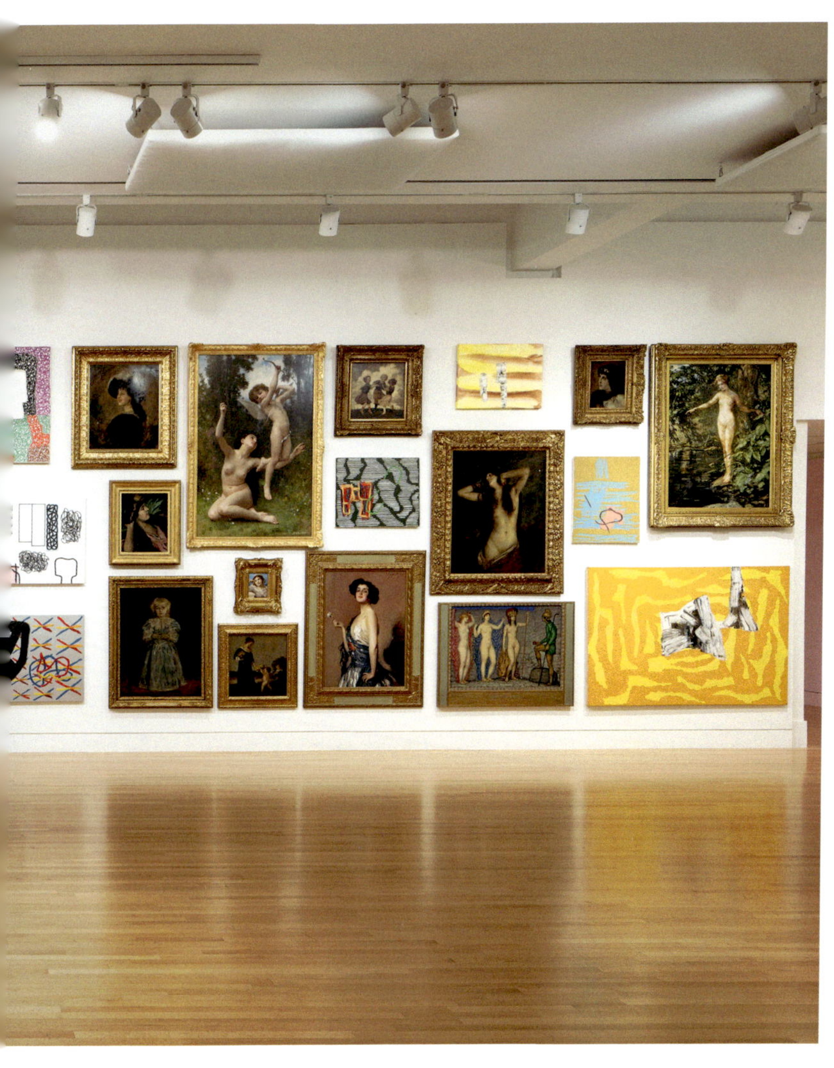

Next spread:
Jonathan Lasker. *Objects Have Reasons* (detail), 2020.
Oil on linen. 30 × 40 in. Courtesy of the artist; Greene Naftali, New York; Thaddaeus Ropac, Paris; and Timothy Taylor, New York.
Photo: Elisabeth Bernstein

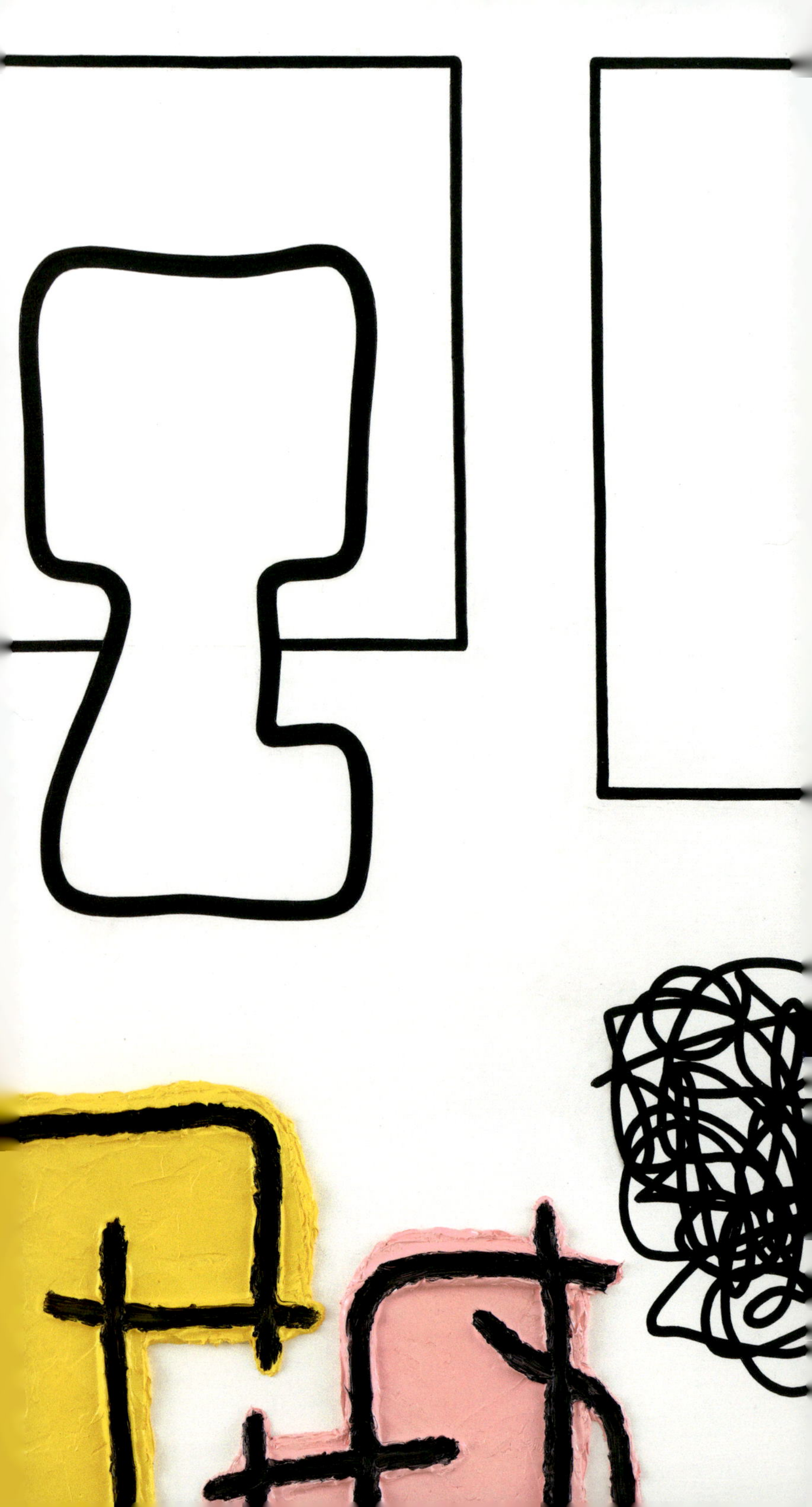

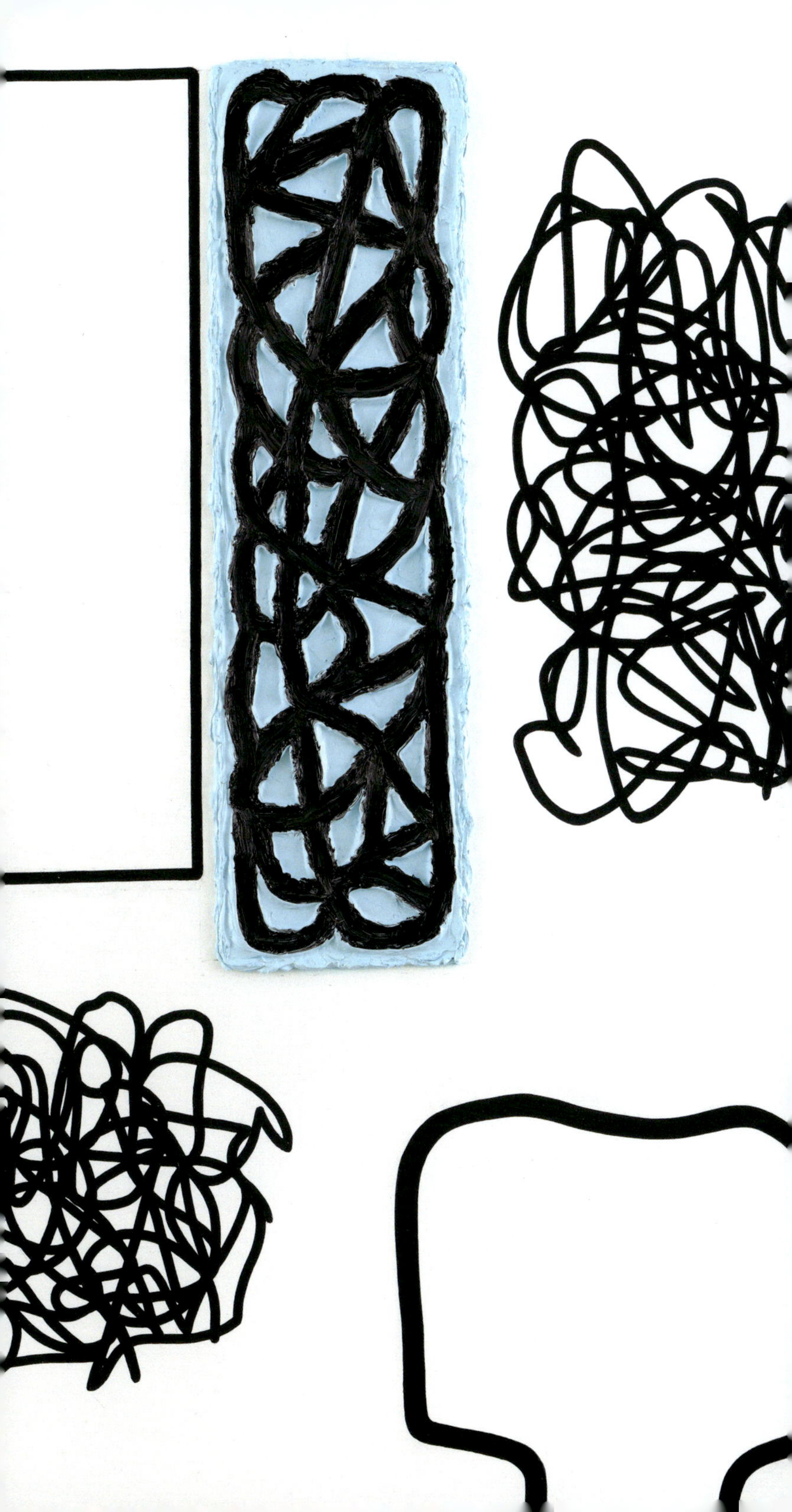

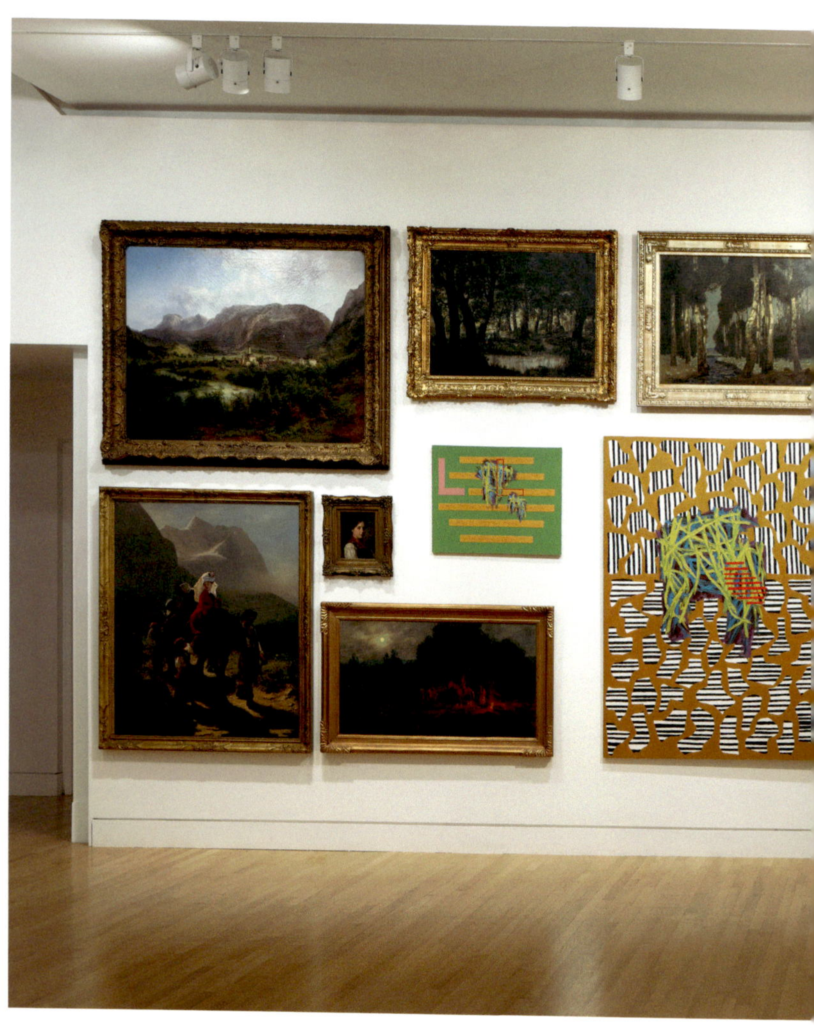

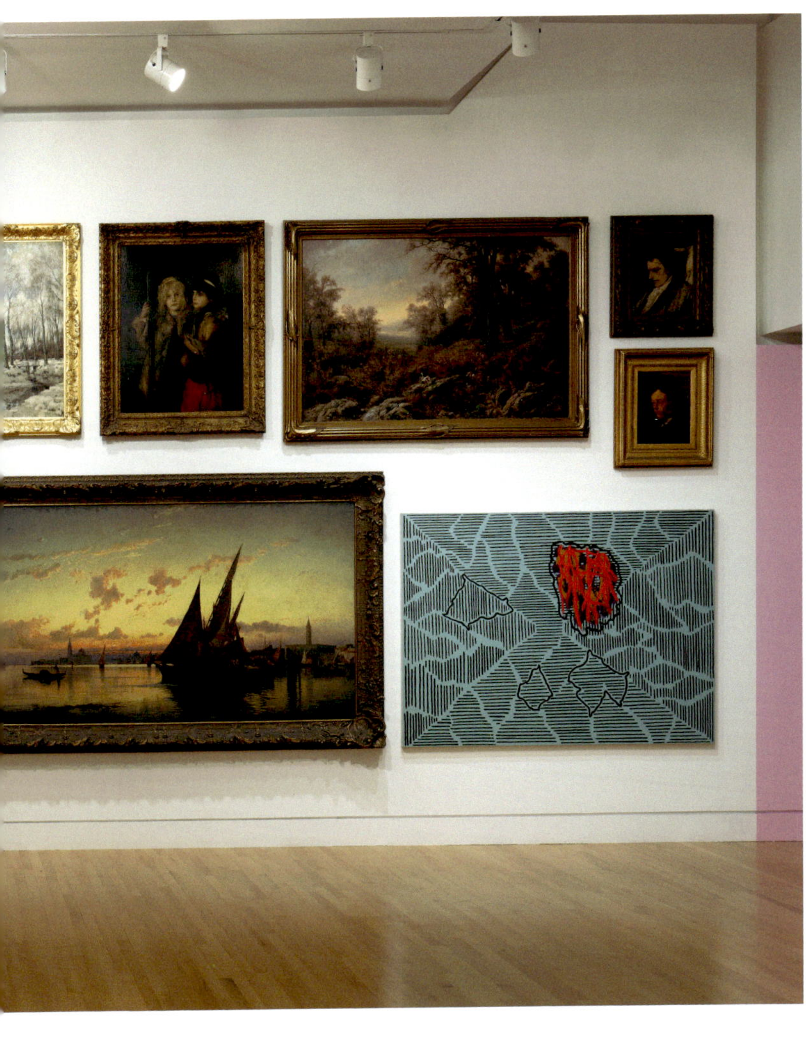

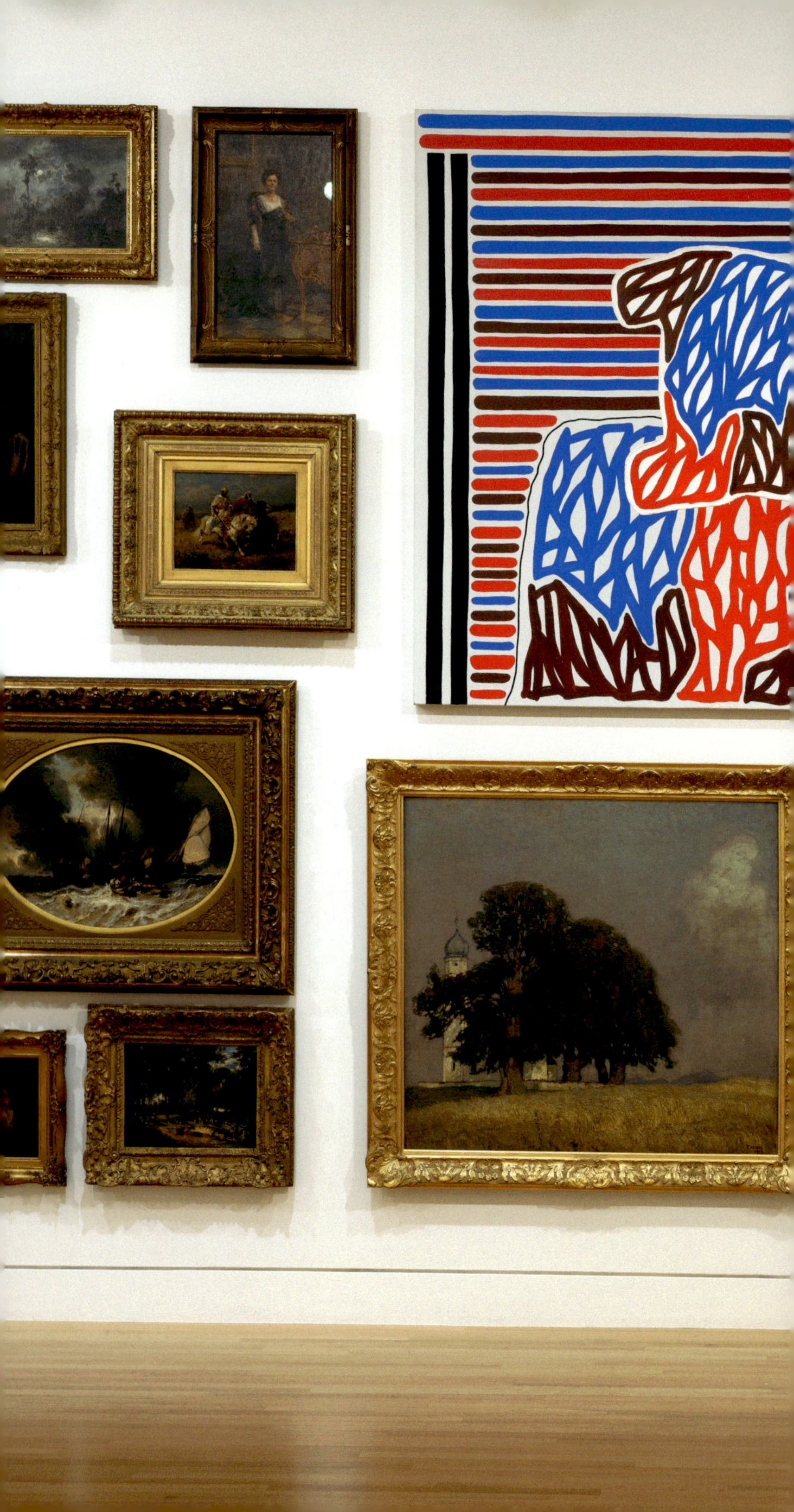

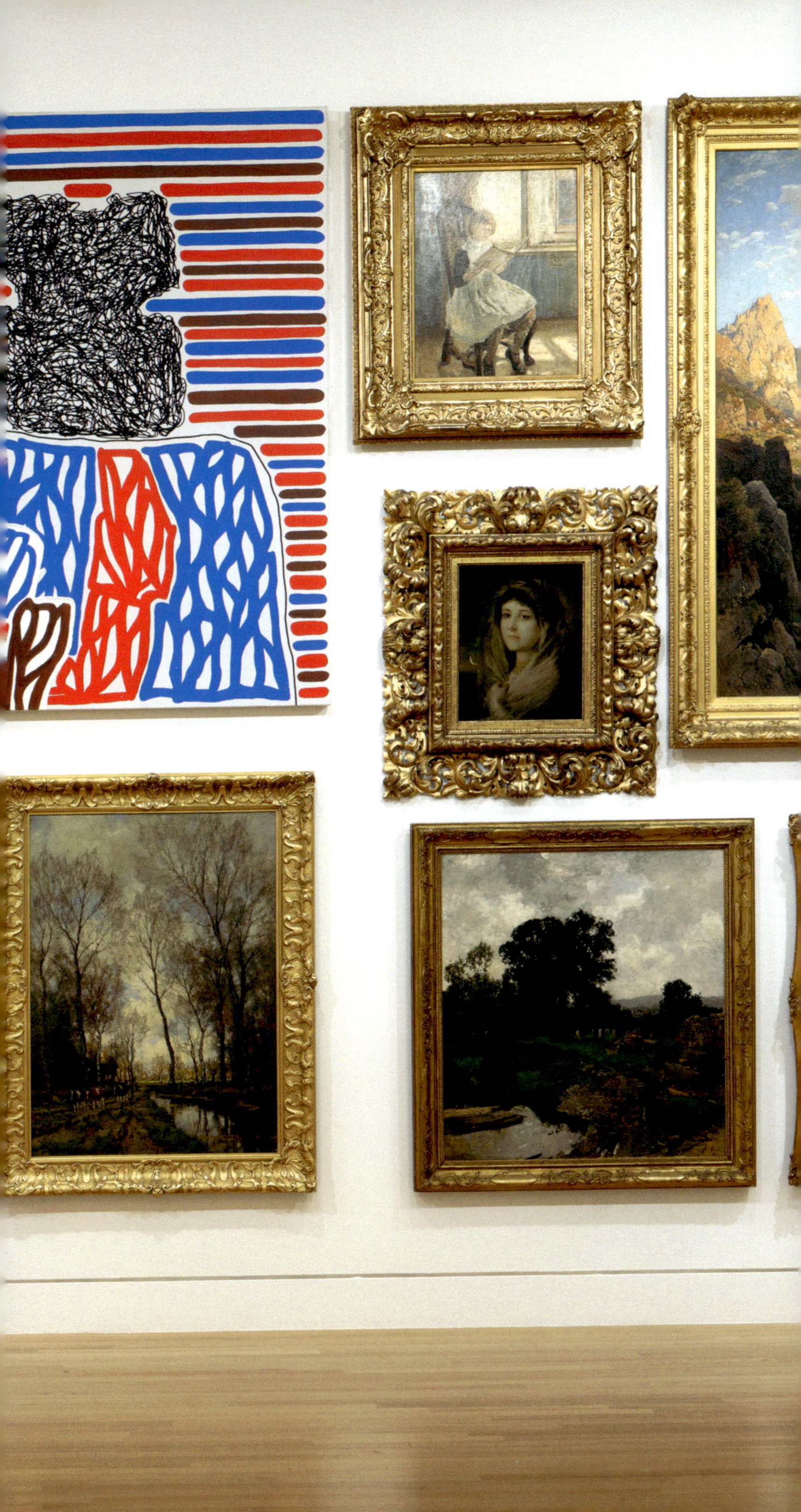

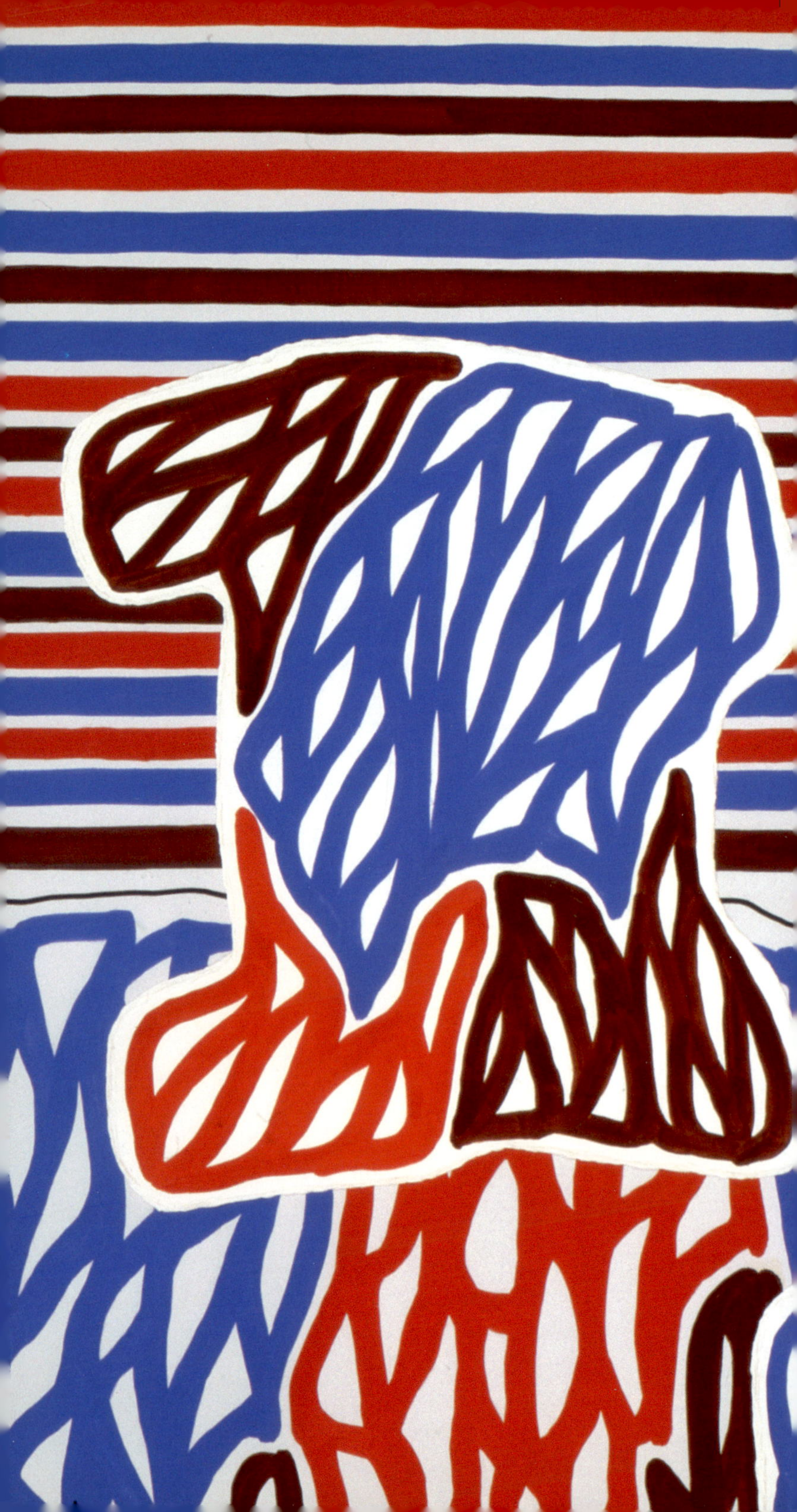

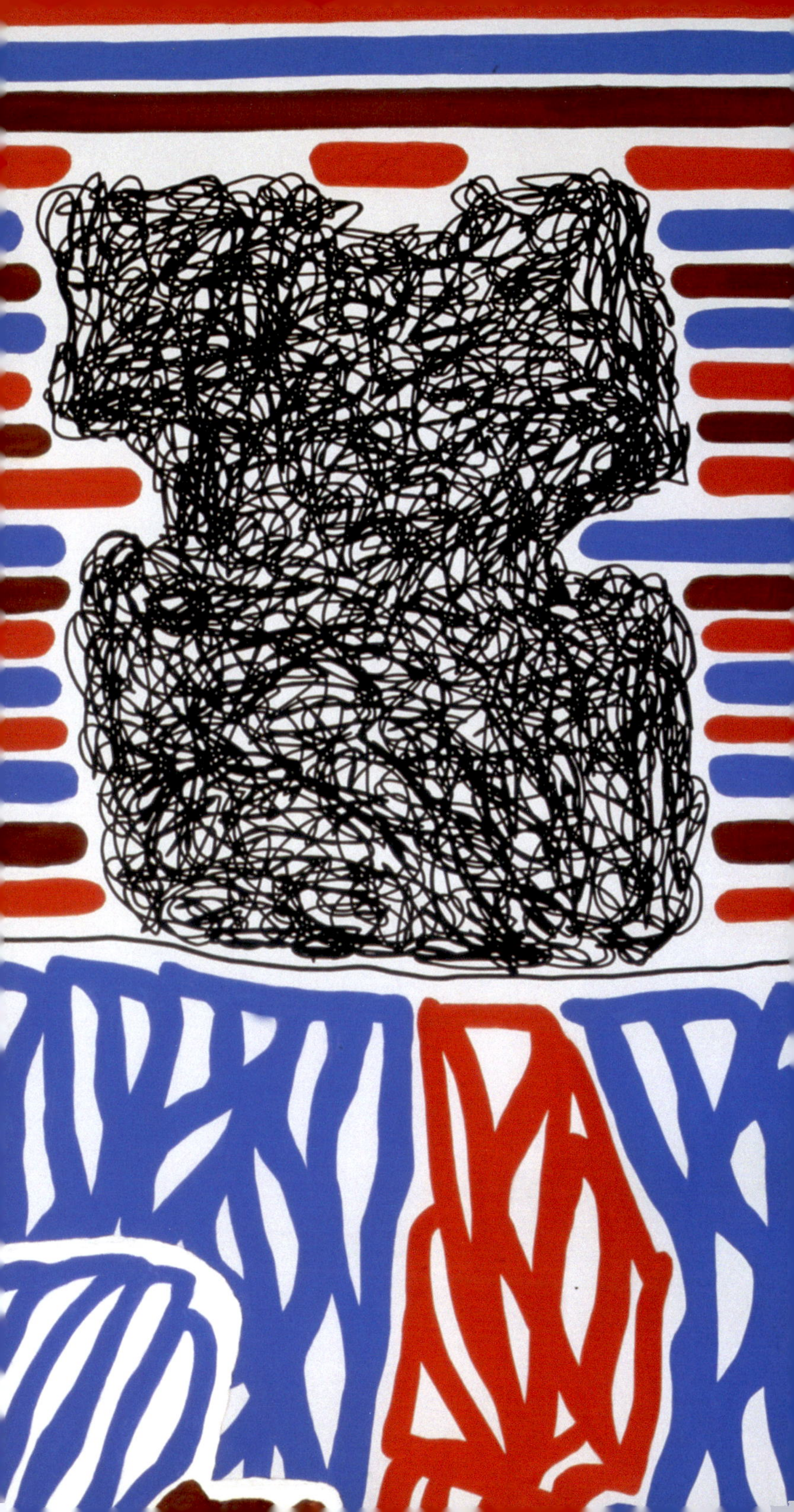

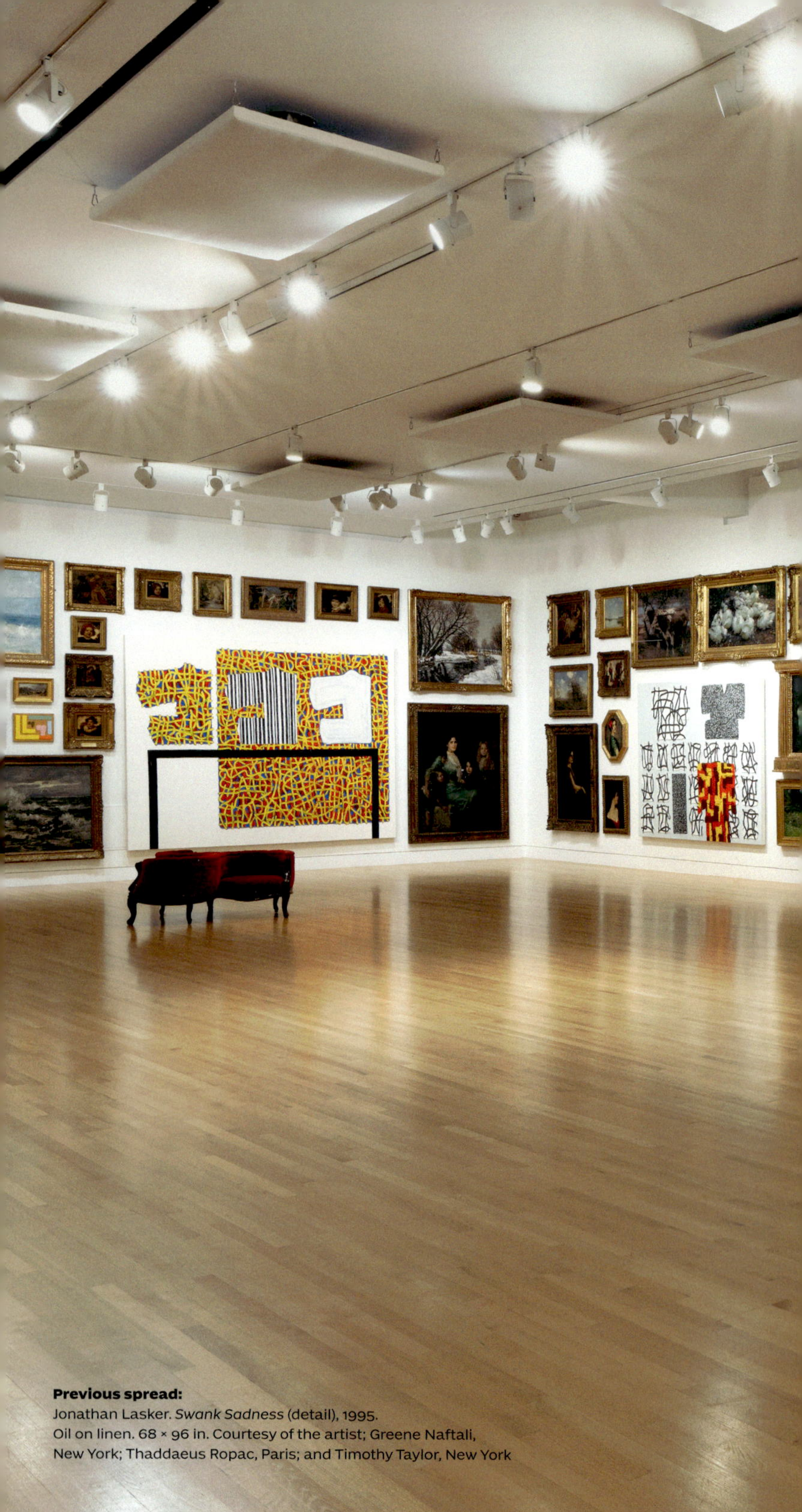

Previous spread:
Jonathan Lasker. *Swank Sadness* (detail), 1995.
Oil on linen. 68 × 96 in. Courtesy of the artist; Greene Naftali, New York; Thaddaeus Ropac, Paris; and Timothy Taylor, New York

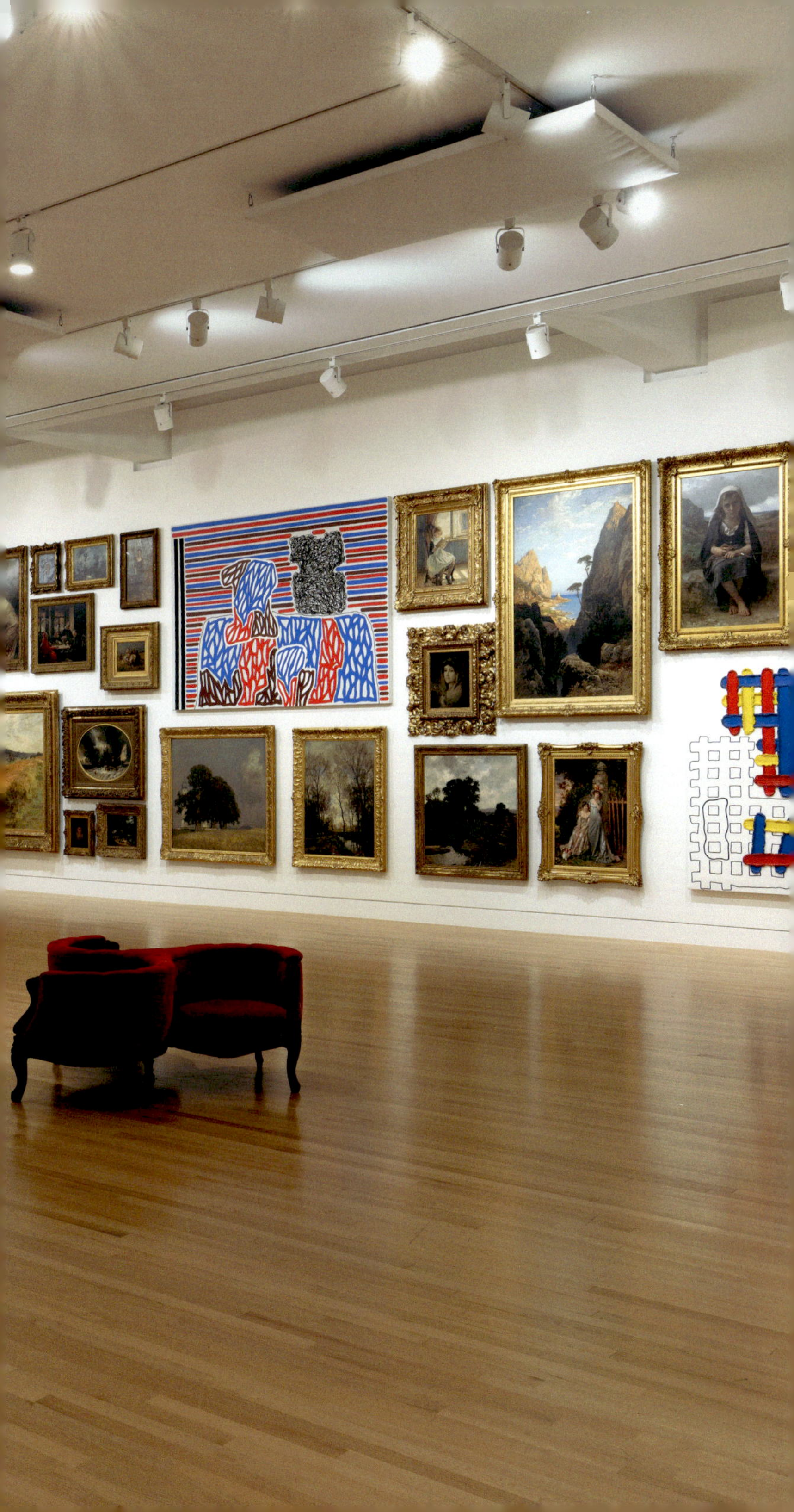

Artist Biography and Exhibition History

Born July 30, 1948, Jersey City, NJ

Lives and works in New York and Munich

Selected Solo Exhibitions

2025 *Frye Salon + Jonathan Lasker* and *Jonathan Lasker: Drawings and Studies*, Frye Art Museum, Seattle

Jonathan Lasker: Pictures for Happy Existentialists, Timothy Taylor, London

2024 *Jonathan Lasker: Paintings from Four Decades*, Muzeul de Artă Recentă, Bucharest, Romania

2023 The LAB, Seattle

Jonathan Lasker: The Life of Objects in a Picture, Greene Naftali, New York

2022 *Jonathan Lasker: New Paintings*, Thaddaeus Ropac, Paris

2019 *Jonathan Lasker: Paintings and Studies for Paintings*, University of the Arts, Philadelphia

2015 *Jonathan Lasker: Paintings 2001–2014*, Musée d'art moderne et contemporain de Saint-Étienne Métropole, France

2008 *Jonathan Lasker*, Portland Art Museum, OR

2005 *Jonathan Lasker: From Drawing to Painting to Drawing*, Kunsthallen Brandts, Odense, Denmark; Pori Art Museum, Finland

2003 *Jonathan Lasker: Paintings, Drawings, Studies 1977–2003*, Palacio de Velázquez, Museo Nacional Centro de Arte Reina Sofía, Madrid; K20 Kunstsammlung Nordrhein-Westfalen, Düsseldorf, Germany

1999–2000 *Jonathan Lasker: Selective Identity–Paintings from the 1990s*, Forum for Contemporary Art, St. Louis; The Power Plant Contemporary Art Gallery, Toronto; Rose Art Museum, Brandeis University, Waltham, MA; Birmingham Museum of Art, AL

1998 *Jonathan Lasker: Paintings 1986–1997*, Centre culturel Nicolas-Pomel and Centre d'art contemporain, Issoire, France

1997–1998 *Jonathan Lasker: Paintings 1977–1997*, Kunsthalle Bielefeld, Germany; Stedelijk Museum, Amsterdam; Kunstverein St. Gallen im Kunstmuseum, Switzerland

1992 *Jonathan Lasker: Paintings 1985–1991*, Institute of Contemporary Art, University of Pennsylvania, Philadelphia

Selected Group Exhibitions

2024 *Pictorial Resonance*, Galerie Thomas Schulte, Berlin

From Gerhard Richter to Mary Heilmann: Abstract Art from Private Collections and the Museum's Holdings, Kunst Museum Winterthur, Switzerland

2023 *The Searchers*, University of the Arts, Philadelphia

Recent Acquisitions, Rollins Museum of Art, Winter Park, FL

New Ground: Jacob Samuel and Contemporary Etching, The Museum of Modern Art, New York

2022 *The Fiction of Property*, Kienzle Art Foundation, Berlin

2020 *Private Eyes, Selections from the Christen Sveaas' Art Foundation*, KODE Art Museum, Bergen, Norway

Au rendez-vous des amis. Modernism in Dialogue with Contemporary Art from the Sammlung Goetz, Pinakothek der Moderne, Munich

2019 *That '80s Show*, Nassau County Museum of Art, Roslyn Harbor, NY

Frozen Gesture, Kunst Museum Winterthur, Switzerland

Legends and Legacy: Revolutions in Hand Papermaking, Rosenwald-Wolf Gallery, University of the Arts, Philadelphia

2018 *I Still Believe in Miracles—Works from the Selvaag Art Collection*, Astrup Fearnley Museet, Oslo

Paintings from the 1980s and 1990s, Musée d'Art Moderne Grand-Duc Jean, Luxembourg City

Summertime Picks, Tamarind Institute, Albuquerque

2017 *Abstract Painting Now!*, Kunsthalle Krems, Krems an der Donau, Austria

Permanent Repetition, Arti et Amicitiae, Amsterdam

Canadian Biennial, National Gallery of Canada, Ottawa

Sammlung Kienzle, Kunstmuseum Liechtenstein, Vaduz

2016 *How to Be Unique*, Kienzle Art Foundation, Berlin

The Conversation Continues: Highlights from the James Cottrell and Joseph Lovett Collection, Orlando Museum of Art, FL

Basquiat, Dubuffet, Soulages . . . Une Collection Privée, Fondation de l'Hermitage, Lausanne, Switzerland

2014 *Drawings and Prints: Selections from the Permanent Collection*, Metropolitan Museum of Art, New York

93 Exhibition, Centro Galego de Arte Contemporánea, Santiago de Compostela, Spain

Busan Biennale 2014, Busan Museum of Art, South Korea

The Hidden Picture – Collecting Art at ING, Cobra Museum voor Moderne Kunst, Amstelveen, the Netherlands

2013 *Wit*, The Painting Center, New York

Entrée Libre Mais Non Obligatoire, Villa Arson, Nice, France

Keine Parole: Aktion-Malerei-Konzept, Werke aus der Sammlung Kienzle, Berlin, Kunstmuseum Kloster Unser Lieben Frauen, Magdeburg, Germany

Promenades d'Amateurs, Nouveau Musée National de Monaco

2012 *American Art of the 1980s*, Nosbaum Reding, Luxembourg City

Art in Embassies Exhibition, US Embassy, Luxembourg City

Conceptual Abstraction, Hunter College, Times Square Gallery, New York

Heute. Malerei, Kunstmuseum Kloster Unser Lieben Frauen, Magdeburg, Germany

2011 *Invitational Exhibition of Visual Arts*, American Academy of Arts and Letters, New York

Exhibition of Newly Elected Members and Recipients of Honors and Awards, American Academy of Arts and Letters, New York

2010 *Loose Joints*, Kienzle Art Foundation, Berlin

Babel, Fonds Régional d'Art Contemporain Auvergne, Clermont-Ferrand, France

Tamarind Touchstones: Fabulous at Fifty, University of New Mexico Art Museum, Albuquerque

Currents in Contemporary Art, Orlando Museum of Art, FL

2009 *Die Gegenwart der Linie*, Staatliche Graphische Sammlung, Pinakothek der Moderne, Munich

Jettison: New Ideas in Abstraction, Trahern Gallery, Austin Peay University, Clarksville, TN

False Friends (Collecting Evidence Part I), Brandenburgischer Kunstverein, Potsdam, Germany

2008 *Out of Storage I: Peintures choisies de la Collection*, Musée d'Art Moderne Grand-Duc Jean, Luxembourg City

En construcción I, La Fundación Pedro Barrié de la Maza, Vigo, Spain

2007 *Nouvelle Présentation des Collections du Musée National d'Art Moderne*, Centre Pompidou, Paris

Conversations: Artist and Collector—The Collection of James Cottrell and Joseph Lovett, North Dakota Museum of Art, Grand Forks

On Paper!: Amerikanische Zeichnung ab 1960, Gesellschaft für Gegenwartskunst, Augsburg, Germany

Articulated Forms, Rabley Contemporary Drawing Center, Marlborough, England

Contemporary, Cool and Collected, Mint Museum of Art, Charlotte, NC

2001 *Between Language and Form*, Yale University Art Gallery, New Haven, CT

1998 *Pop/Abstraction*, Pennsylvania Academy of the Fine Arts, Philadelphia

1993 *The Permanent Collection Revisited*, Hirshhorn Museum and Sculpture Garden, Washington, DC

1989 *Horn of Plenty*, Stedelijk Museum, Amsterdam

1985 *Vernacular Abstraction*, Wacoal Art Center, Tokyo

Selected Professional Awards

2011 American Academy of Arts and Letters, New York, Arts and Letters Award

2000 Honorary Visiting Professorship, The London Institute

1989 National Endowment for the Arts Fellowship Grant

1989 New York Foundation for the Arts Fellowship Grant

1987 National Endowment for the Arts Fellowship Grant

Selected Collections

Birmingham Museum of Art, AL
Buffalo AKG Art [AKG Art Museum] Museum, NY
High Museum of Art, Atlanta
Hirshhorn Museum and Sculpture Garden, Washington, DC
Los Angeles County Museum of Art
Metropolitan Museum of Art, New York
Moderna Museet, Stockholm
Musée d'Art Moderne Grand-Duc Jean, Luxembourg City
Musée National d'Art Moderne, Centre Pompidou, Paris
Musée d'art moderne et contemporain de Saint-Étienne Métropole, France
Museo Nacional Centro de Arte Reina Sofía, Madrid
Museum Ludwig, Cologne
Museum of Fine Arts, Houston
National Gallery of Art, Washington, DC
National Gallery of Canada, Ottawa
The Museum of Modern Art, New York
Wacoal Art Center, Tokyo
Whitney Museum of American Art, New York

Education

1977 California Institute of the Arts, Valencia, CA

1975–77 School of Visual Arts, New York

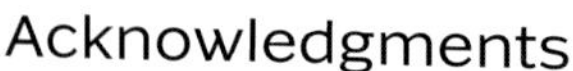
Acknowledgments

Frye Salon + Jonathan Lasker reflects the legacy of Charles and Emma Frye's collection as a catalyst for fostering dialogue between the art of our founders' time and ours. Inviting Jonathan Lasker's work into *Frye Salon* creates a physical bridge between past and present meanings of the Frye within the greater Seattle community and beyond. We look forward to continuing such interventions that support the museum as a destination for the exchange of unexpected ideas and diverse viewpoints. We are most grateful to the Fryes for the model of enduring support for art and artists they established.

Many individuals worked in support of this project. We convey our heartfelt thanks first and foremost to Jonathan Lasker for bringing his integral contributions to the legacy of Postmodern painting to the Frye. The museum is honored by the opportunity to consider our collection in conversation with the questions Lasker's work raises, not only around space and movement, but also of what a painting can be. Exhibiting his artwork here invigorates our walls and our minds.

We are grateful to Faith Brower, director and curator of collections, for her superb oversight of *Frye Salon + Jonathan Lasker* and its companion exhibition, *Jonathan Lasker: Drawings and Studies.*

Frye Salon + Jonathan Lasker came to fruition through the contributions of the museum's expert staff and contracted colleagues, whose names appear near the building's entrance and on page 60 of this book. We also are grateful to our board of trustees for supporting our work instigating fresh conversations and perspectives around the museum's collection.

We extend profound thanks to Jeff and Judy Greenstein for their valued partnership and generosity in lending multiple artworks to the exhibition. The Greensteins' assistant, Lyda Barr, must also be acknowledged for the invaluable support she provided. We are also very grateful to Greene Naftali and Timothy Taylor for lending works to the exhibition, along with their expertise.

The staff of Marquand Books were instrumental in realizing the vision of this publication, most notably Olivia Atmore, Gina Broze, Leah Finger, and Kestrel Rundle. We also extend many thanks to copy editor Kathleen Garrett and proofreader Emily Holt for their careful, thoughtful work. A special thanks is owed to Marquand Books's design director, Tom Eykemans, for his astute design of this book. We are deeply appreciative of Frye graphic designer, Lexi McCauley, for creating a perfect exhibition identity for *Frye Salon + Jonathan Lasker* and to our ace editorial projects team, Jennifer Cha, Laura Landau, and Erin Langner, for ensuring our high-quality publications program.

We thank the following individuals and institutions for their support in securing the rights and reproductions that were instrumental to this publication: Diana Edkins, Art Resource, New York; M. Fernanda Pessaro, Artists Rights Society (ARS), New York; Bénédicte Burrus and Ashley Giahn, Galerie Thaddaeus Ropac, Paris; Ryan Miller and Cory Nomura, Greene Naftali, New York; Jessica Jernigan, Modern Art Museum of Fort Worth; Geneviève Daigneault, National Gallery of Canada, Ottawa; Daniel Polonsky, Petzel Gallery, New York; Claire Corridon, Sperone Westwater, New York; and Louise Burley, Tate Images, London. We are also grateful to Jueqian Fang for her impeccable photographs of the exhibition.

Finally, we acknowledge that none of what we do at the Frye Art Museum would be possible if not for the Coast Salish peoples, specifically the Duwamish and Suquamish Tribes, who have since time immemorial stewarded the lands and waters of this place we now call Seattle. We offer gratitude and respect to their elders past and present, as well as to future generations for their continued stewardship.

Jamilee Lacy
Executive Director
Frye Art Museum

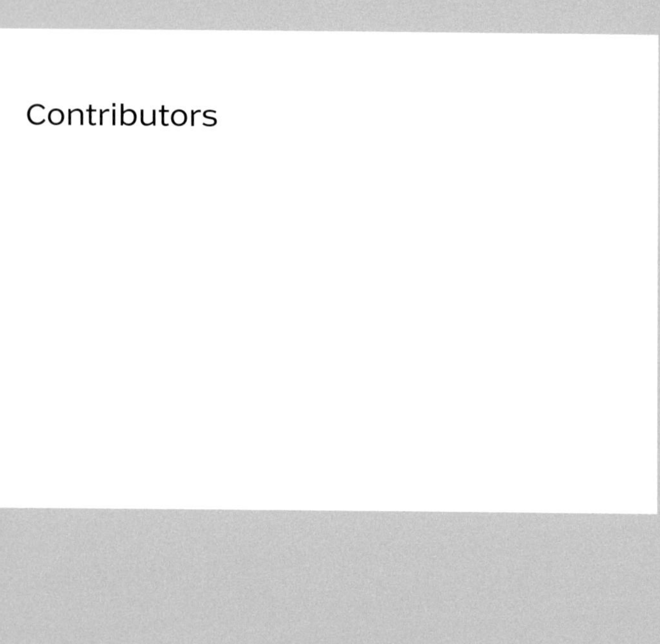
Contributors

Jeff and Judy Greenstein
Jeff and Judy Greenstein are collectors of postwar modern and contemporary art. Their collection focuses on established artists who have dedicated their careers to exploring abstraction.

Jamilee Lacy
Jamilee Lacy is executive director of the Frye Art Museum, where she established the Local Ties collecting initiative, minted the Frye Parlor site-specific art series, and commissioned a major redesign of the museum café by the international artist-run atelier Print Club. Lacy previously served as inaugural director and chief curator of Providence College Galleries, where she organized dozens of contemporary art exhibitions and projects, including with Sanford Biggers, Edie Fake, and Sheida Soleimani. Lacy was also a 2022 Fellow at the Center for Curatorial Leadership.

This book is published in conjunction with the exhibition *Frye Salon + Jonathan Lasker*, organized by the Frye Art Museum, Seattle, and presented at the Frye, October 25, 2025–September 20, 2026.

The exhibition and publication are made possible with generous support from Frye Members. Seasonal support provided by 4Culture.

ISBN: 978-1-64657-047-8
Library of Congress Control Number: 2025938540

Frye Art Museum
704 Terry Avenue
Seattle, WA 98104
USA
www.fryemuseum.org

Available through:
ARTBOOK | D.A.P.
75 Broad Street, Suite 630
New York, NY 10004
www.artbook.com

Produced by Marquand Books, Seattle
www.marquandbooks.com

Design by Thomas Eykemans
Exhibition identity design by Lexi McCauley
Copyedited by Kathleen Garrett
Proofread by Emily Holt
Typeset in Riggs and Murtaugh by Maggie Lee
Color separations by I/O Color, Seattle
Printed and bound by Artron Art Group, China

Cover and back cover: Installation views of *Frye Salon + Jonathan Lasker*, Frye Art Museum, Seattle, October 25, 2025–September 20, 2026. Photos: Jueqian Fang

FRYE ART MUSEUM

Board of Trustees

Staff